CW00538658

PRAISE FOR *THE DEFINITIVE GL*
BUDGET APPRⱯVᴄᴅ!

❝ Great book I highly recommend it. As a Senior Consultant I have been reading so many useless books about new methods for improving Business Cases, but this one finally establishes the value for my customer.❞

> Pat Dugan,
> *Xerox Global Services,*
> *Managing Principal,*
> *Rochester, New York, USA*

❝ That book is great! In my domain it is really difficult to quantify intangible benefits such as customer satisfaction and quality. Now, I finally found a practical approach to do just that!❞

> Alan Martin,
> *Agilent, Business*
> *Development Manager, Love-*
> *land, Colorado, USA*

❝ I've been a marketing professor for 20 years now but there has never been a clear and concise description of a scientific method about how to measure soft benefits of marketing campaigns, until now! Thanks to The Definitive Guide to Getting Your Budget Approved I´m now able to calculate the value of new marketing campaigns in Euros and Cents. This book comes with a library of practical examples, is easy to read and an outstanding guideline to quantify qualitative values! That is why I also advice this book to my students about how to develop a proper Business Case for upcoming marketing actions. Great job guys!❞

> Gert-Jan Hummel,
> *Stenden University,*
> *Marketing Professor,*
> *Emmen, Netherlands*

" The described methodology is the best for the measurement of soft benefits currently available. Frank and Johannes do an excellent job of explaining how to measure qualitative values such as quality, innovation, information accuracy and customer satisfaction. I regularly use this method to demonstrate the hidden values of the SAS Business Intelligence Solution to my customers. In cases where we follow this method strictly during the sales process, the sales people were able to improve their close ratio tremendously and increase their income."

> Andreas Gödde,
> *SAS Institute, Director*
> *Business Intelligence,*
> *Heidelberg, Germany*

" This book is quite an eye opener. It not merely reveals the importance of intangible benefits, but clearly explains how to measure them. As a Divisional Director I depend on true-to-life methods and this book finally represents a helpful guideline for the measurement of soft benefits!"

> Jesper Schleimann,
> *SAP,*
> *Divisional Director,*
> *Copenhagen, Denmark*

" As director of Emmtec Services I have to put a focus on soft benefits, which get more and more important in today's business. If I am not able to differentiate our industry- and business park from others, I will not be competitive anymore in the following years. The Definitive Guide to Getting Your Budget Approved is of great help to calculate and measure these soft benefits and therefore to gain a competitive advantage! Thanks to Johannes' and Frank's method the value of projects with qualitative values can be expressed in Euros and Cents. This simplifies the justification of an investment and leads to a higher win rate."

> Rolf van der Mark,
> *Emmtec Services BV, Director, Emmen, Netherlands*

About the Authors

Johannes Ritter is Partner at Solution Matrix and is a leading authority on Business Case methodology. He has worked with some of the leading companies in 20 countries on the successful deployment of Business Cases.

Johannes brings practical best practice techniques for modeling key business drivers, critical success factors, and business objectives on large, complex business projects. With a wide range of Business Case experience, from simple 1 million Euro to complex 250 million Euro outsourcing contracts, Johannes has helped dozens of teams in banking, energy, insurance, IT, manufacturing, public sector, and telecommunications in making better investment decisions.

Frank Röttgers is a consultant with Solution Matrix, a consulting firm focused on Business Case Analysis tools, training, and resources for building the financial Business Case. Frank has worked with a wide range of functional groups from sales to IT to engineering on how to analyze, build, and present Business Cases with primarily qualitative benefits. Amongst others, he developed Business Cases for companies such as KLM Royal Dutch Airlines, Tesco, and SAS. Within the framework of these projects he measured soft benefits such as quality, image, innovation, return on health, and customer satisfaction. Guess what! Qualitative values are worth millions!

We dedicate this book to our families,
Irmela von Baross, Sabine Ritter-von Baross,
Jonatan Ritter, Wolfgang Ritter, Maria Röttgers,
Dirk Röttgers (Erster...), and Johannes Röttgers for
providing the wind beneath our wings.

The Definitive Guide to
Getting Your Budget Approved!

Measure Intangibles to Calculate
Your ROI Business Case

JOHANNES RITTER & FRANK RÖTTGERS

International Standard Book Number: 978-3-00-026307-1

Library of Congress Control Number: 2010-916822

Library of Congress subject headings:

Budget
Business – Decision making
Business – Simulation methods
Cost benefit analysis – Methods
Monte Carlo method
Monte Carlo simulation
Project management – Cost effectiveness
Project management – Decision making
Project management – Finance
Return on Investment
Risk management

Design: www.envinion.com

First Publishing: January 2011

▓ CONTENT AT A GLANCE

▨ TABLE OF CONTENTS

■ TABLE OF CONTENTS

Foreword

Since the time of Jules Dupuit (1804-1866) to the current day, the concept of investment has been supported by structured methods. Despite the strong advances in theory and practice over this time, the same fundamental questions concerning benefits and risks are on the agenda. Globalization has increased competition, which has promoted the quest for optimal gains and led to the advancement of services and technical resources. The concept of the Business Case has therefore become fundamental. In order to control risk, the Business Case addresses the required study material to be selected, organized, analyzed, recommended and approved (or not). Indeed, the Business Case is a tool package which provides a summary of a context and scenarios analyzed quantitatively and qualitatively with recommendations that are necessary in making an informed investment decision.

This book is organized around describing the soft benefits of the Business Case. As its title purports: "The Definitive Guide to Getting Your Budget Approved! Measure Intangibles to Calculate Your ROI Business Case" meets the expectations of the operational practitioners tasked with managing and delivering projects. The succinct text contains the knowledge necessary, combining neoclassic economic theory with specific methods, to understand and practice the configuration of a financial model that allows the quantification of qualitative values. Current reference manuals in the market are very complete, with associated theoretical analysis. However, they are not synthesized into an accessible format for the practitioner and so this book attempts to fulfill this need. Through the course of the book, the authors make reference to professional practice and real-world situations that provide the reader with a firsthand eyewitness account of application of methods. With the "barber" example, the authors demonstrate a pedagogic effort to teach practically and thus achieve maximum understanding.

The main purpose of the book is therefore to propose an approach to practitioners who need to find and develop a capital budget, through having realistic and effective approaches that are applicable to everyday working situations. For instance, the guidance material will facilitate the creation of Influence Matrices outlining one or more goals and scenarios. Examples will guide us to build a financial model with software tools such as Excel. Furthermore, basic techniques to manage the uncertainty of risk will be presented. The book is rooted in both the experience of finance gained by the authors in prestigious international companies but also through their teaching experience and training seminars. It is reader-friendly and performs an important contribution to all the types of debates and concerns faced by both investors and project managers. It explains the modern form of quantifying the qualitative values taking into account the aspect of risk analysis, something which is not very common in the economic literature.

The key message of the book is that the business world is changing. Management tools have been afforded new dimensions, opening the possibility for them to be exported from their current application domains and made more accessible to all. In this context, with an approach that is applicable to all sectors of business, this book is therefore an excellent first step in learning how to value a project.

Jean-Philippe Sendat, MBA
Senior Economist and Financial Analyst
Boeing Research & Technology Europe

Acknowledgements

We did not really think it's already time to write this book. It's the book that wanted to be written. In fact, the content of this book was developed over many years in our seminars and in consulting projects the book wrote itself. So many people helped make this book happen that naming them all is impossible. Nevertheless, we don't want to leave some of them unacknowledged.

We thank our friends, who spent time with us when we needed distance from writing and didn't complain when we haven't had time since we were busy writing.

We thank all our seminar attendees, supporters, colleagues, and advisors: Dr. Marty J. Schmidt, President and Founder Solution Matrix for providing us with the opportunity to work at Solution Matrix. Our colleagues Claudia Assmuth, for her research; Emmanuelle Carandanis for her clever analyses; Nadia Cuesta García, for being the perfectionist and telecommunication expert; Dr. Doris Dehn, for her intellectual rigor and arguing all night long until getting her will; Julia Knapp, for countless hours of reviewing; Christine Marburger, for her sharp mind and never ending enthusiasm; Dominic McCarthy, for his deep knowledge of modeling and statistical intricacies; Franziska Luisa Ochs, for being the free and ironic spirit, and Christian Schaefer for cutting edge web design.

We also thank Dr. Dr. Arndt Künnecke, Dr. Eva Henriette Keller, and Michael Schulte for their legal advice.

The force behind any business is the client, and we have been privileged to work with a number of people, providing us with seemingly impossible challenges and projects. We thank all of them for sharing the journey to their solution with us especially.

And finally, dear reader, we thank you for sharing your time with us. Our wish is to provide you with an applicable book and we hope that you can make use of its contents.

Anything you need to quantify can be measured in some way that is superior to not measuring it at all.

— Gilb's Law

Preface

This book illustrates how qualitative values in your business projects and investment opportunities can be quantified in monetary terms by making use of Business Case Analysis to get your budget approved. It describes the theory of how to measure intangible benefits and uses customer satisfaction as a practical example.

A few years ago so called "soft benefits" such as customer satisfaction, image, quality or innovation were only perceived, but not really taken into consideration while making crucial business decisions. Nowadays such qualitative values play one of the most important roles when trying to differentiate from competitors and deliver an added value to the customer. Owing to this, more and more organizations strive to change their measurement of qualitative benefits. Instead of measuring their qualitative values in terms of "good", "average", and "bad", they want to quantify their qualitative values in monetary terms. Expressing qualitative values in currency enables organizations to compare apples with apples. When two different projects compete for the same funds, steering committees are often inclined to favor the investment where the benefits are not of a qualitative type.[1] This is because a number such as "1,000,000 € increase in revenue" is easier to grasp and to imagine than "15% increase in customer satisfaction". But what if these 15% increase in customer satisfaction is worth more than 1,000,000 €? Possessing the ability to quantify qualitative values in monetary terms enables you to compare the benefits of such investments, make appropriate decisions, and get your budget approved.

The quantification of qualitative values is getting more and more important in today's business world. However, there is a lack of knowledge within many organizations about how to do so. This is a result of the belief that intangibles are immeasurable and therefore not quantifiable in

---

1 Cf. Schmidt, 2002, p. 1.

monetary terms. This book not only provides evidence that it is possible to quantify such qualitative values in monetary terms but also reveals you how to do so. The approach used within this book is divided into three steps. These steps will be illustrated by using a practical example, in which the qualitative value – customer satisfaction – is quantified in monetary terms.

The first step to quantify qualitative values is visualizing the decision problem with an Influence Matrix. During our public seminars a lot of clients state that their main problem is the complexity of their case. Creating an Influence Matrix solves this problem by decomposing complex problems into quantifiable elements. This is achieved by dividing the problem into values, scenarios, decisions, and uncertainties. An Influence Matrix, which includes every relevant element of the decision problem, is the foundation for the quantification of a qualitative value.

The second step is to quantify the elements of the decision problem by creating the financial model. The way the elements of the Influence Matrix are arranged gives the financial model its structure. After structuring the financial model, the dependencies and relationships between the elements of the decision problem are converted into formulas. When the financial model is completed, the data for the specific elements of the problem need to be collected. This is done by interviewing subject matter experts.

The third step is to analyze the results of the financial model by performing a sensitivity analysis. One element of performing the sensitivity analysis is analyzing the probability of the outcomes of the financial model. This is done by setting up a Monte Carlo simulation, which provides you with a probability density function from which the likelihood of the results can be read off. Carrying out a sensitivity analysis also provides you with the information about what the biggest risk factors are and their impact on the project.

Applying this approach and using these tools allows you to compare investments. The 15% increase in customer satisfaction from the example can be quantified into a monetary value and directly compared to the 1,000,000 € increase in revenue. Therefore the quantification of qualitative value leads to better decisions and to getting your budget approved.

A Business Case is the Key
to Quantify Qualitative Values

Imagine a business world in which you are able to measure qualitative benefits such as customer satisfaction, image, quality or innovation in monetary terms. What is wrong with this picture? "Such benefits are intangible, immeasurable, and therefore cannot be quantified in monetary terms" is an often heard phrase during our seminars *www.business-case-seminar.com*. We say the only thing that is wrong with this picture is that you do not have to imagine such a business world, because it already exists.

Our experience shows that steering committees often categorically reject investment projects where the benefits are primarily qualitative or "soft", such as "increased customer satisfaction" or "an improved image". This is not just due to the fact that project leaders were not able to quantify such values, but rather the belief that such things cannot possibly be quantified at all. As a consequence of not even meeting the challenge to quantify qualitative values, many organizations misallocate resources, reject good, and accept bad investments. In other words money is wasted because in today's organizations there is an inability to quantify qualitative values in monetary terms, which leads to higher costs.

The reason why this is an alarming problem is evident. In the past it was easy to run a business by simply calculating and analyzing the quantitative values such as amount of products, production costs and selling price. Nowadays however, due to globalization, competition is increasing and it is hard for every business to gain a competitive advantage. One way left to differentiate oneself from the competition is to concentrate on and specialize in qualitative values such as customer satisfaction, which will be used as a practical example throughout this book.

Particularly with regard to marketing the last few years have shown an increased necessity to quantify qualitative values since more and more of an organization's assets consist of qualitative values instead of quantitative values. The recent outsourcing of DELL's service hotline to India is just one example of what can happen if qualitative values are not taken into consideration when making important business decisions. While the decreased costs are easily recognized, the decreased worker productivity and quality are more subtle. The erosion of quality is not evident until a company, such as DELL, is faced with massive consumer complaints about lackluster customer service.

From a decision-maker's point of view, the problem to quantify qualitative values results from its complexity. They argue that there is a huge amount of internal and external factors that can have influence on a qualitative value such as customer satisfaction. Even when they are able to point out all the relevant factors, they still face the problem of quantifying them. In the end they do not even try to overcome this inability to quantify qualitative values, which would in turn allow them to gain a competitive advantage.

However, the problem that qualitative values are hard to quantify is not as complex as it might seem. It is just about using the right approach in combination with suitable tools. Instead of discussing Business Case Analysis theoretically, this book will concentrate on why and how to apply Business Case Analysis to practical examples. In order to do so, Chapter I will cover the first step on the path by introducing the Influence Matrix, a tool used to visualize a decision problem. Chapter II will then show why and how to use financial modeling to quantify the elements used within the Influence Matrix. To identify risk factors within the quantification of qualitative values, sensitivity analysis is introduced in Chapter III. Reading this book will provide you with a theoretical grounding and will illustrate a practical application using customer satisfaction as an example of quantifying qualitative values in monetary terms.

PART I

The Influence Matrix Visualizes the Decision Problem

Business Case Analysis provides a step-by-step procedure that has proved practical in tackling even the most complex problems in an efficient and orderly way. Using Business Case Analysis is an excellent approach when beginning with the quantification of qualitative values. It provides a number of tools that can help to analyze decision problems, particularly when you are struggling with a complex set of interactions. One of these tools is the Influence Matrix.

The Influence Matrix visualizes every factor and uncertainty involved in the decision problem and demonstrates the relationships between them. Since one of the biggest problems when quantifying qualitative values in monetary terms is to handle all involved uncertainties within the decision-making process, the Influence Matrix is the most appropriate tool. It is not only a concise statement of the problem, but it also gives you a valuable tool to structure the problem and to discover the assessments and data necessary to analyze the uncertainties.

To illustrate how the Influence Matrix, the financial model, and the tornado diagram work, the underlying theory will be applied to a practical example. The example will demonstrate step-by-step how to quantify the qualitative value customer satisfaction into monetary terms. Although the example will only consider quantifying customer satisfaction for one specific case, the given theory is applicable and adaptable to a broad range of quantification of any qualitative value. For a library of Influence Matrices see Appendix I.

The case study is as follows: One day at lunch we noticed that near our office a lot of hair dressers were opening new shops. We wondered if any of them makes money due to the increasing competition. We made a bet on their profitability and talked to some of them about this. The conversations revealed that customer satisfaction are the magic words to be competitive and profitable further on. To our surprise the issues were similar to our consulting engagements so we picked this as a simple case study. Imagine:

A barber with a medium sized barbershop takes a look at his customer data, of which he keeps track using a paper appointment book and a PC with a spreadsheet program. He recognizes declining customer visits during the last half year. After analyzing the collected customer data, the barber supposes that he constantly loses customers to the new barbershop in town, which opened a few months ago. The barber knows that his and the prices of the new barbershop do not differ. As a result, there has to be another explanation why his customers search for an alternative.

The barber has to admit that lately he has not done any marketing campaigns to attract new customers nor anything proactive to retain his long-term customers. For that reason he suggests that the decline of customer visits during the last half year results from decreased customer satisfaction. Knowing that the decline will not end until he improves his service in a certain way, the barber starts to think about how he would be able to win back his old and additionally can gain new customers.

The only question he asks himself is: "How can I possibly measure the increase of my customers' satisfaction due to a marketing campaign in monetary terms?". It is evident that some marketing campaign has to be done to stop the decline of customer visits, but the problem of finding out and measuring the effect of such a marketing campaign seems to be even harder. The first major problem the barber faces is the complexity of his situation.

CHAPTER I

The Influence Matrix Decomposes Complex Problems

Decision problems are usually complicated and complex. In most cases it is also unclear what the actual problem is and what decisions need to be made. We often observe project teams spending hours on talking about details before having a clearly stated problem definition. In the end these projects fail due to disunity amongst the team members about the actual problem. Fortunately the spirit of Business Case Analysis is to divide and conquer. The dividing is carried out via the Influence Matrix, which breaks down complex problems into quantifiable elements in a concise way. Often the Influence Matrix reveals that you know more about the so called "intangible problem" than you thought you knew before constructing an Influence Matrix.

Decomposition of a complex problem into quantifiable elements means to deconstruct all uncertain elements into constituent parts to identify directly observable elements that are easier to measure than the uncertain element itself. Thus, the more a complicated and complex problem can be split up into a sequence of interrelated factors and causal links, the more effective the analysis becomes. However, an over decomposed problem may confuse more than it clarifies. Therefore, you should be sure not to over decompose the problem if there is a simpler way. Additionally, you should distinguish between two different types of complexity when analyzing the problem: organizational and analytical complexity.

▓ THE COMPLEXITY IS OF AN ORGANIZATIONAL AND ANALYTICAL NATURE

Organizational complexity results from the number of people and organizational units involved in the decision process. The more departments are involved in the process, the more complexity, because all values, desires, and motivations of each participant have to be considered. Additionally, different initial convictions, several fundamental frames, various personalities, and competencies not to mention their different degrees of power and resources need to be taken into consideration. Analytical complexity arises from factors every decision-maker has to deal with. These factors are for example uncertainty, interrelated factors, dynamic relationship between uncertainties and decisions, multiple decision alternatives etc. Since the goal of this book is to provide you with a theoretical grounding and practical application, which will enable you to quantify qualitative values, the practical example will focus on analytical complexity only. Most decision-makers are struggling with this kind of complexity, because they are not able to name or grasp how the analytical complexity arises and how to decompose it for further decision-making.

▓ CAPTURE ANALYTICAL COMPLEXITY AND STRUCTURE IT

In our experience, decision-makers often give up on a problem before they even start to analyze it due to its complexity. However, there are four useful assumptions, which should convince you to at least give it a try. First, the problem is not as unique as you might think. Second, you have more data than you think. Third, you need less data than you might think and fourth, there is a useful measurement that is much simpler than you might think.

Keeping these four important assumptions in mind you are also able to answer the question whether or not the overall objective is tangible. Moreover, the barber from our example asked himself if it is possible to quantify customer satisfaction at all. Using the so called clarification chain answers this question easily. The chain consists of three simple rules:

1. If it matters at all, it is detectable/observable.

2. If it is detectable, it can be detected as an amount (or range of possible amounts).

3. If it can be detected as a range of possible amounts, it can be quantified.

Decision-makers tend to ignore intangibles because there is no clear definition what i.e. quality, image or customer satisfaction in their projects' context means and to what extent it contributes to the organizations' objective. Define the objective properly and the way to success is paved, or as Kettering says: "A problem well stated is a problem half solved"[2].

After defining the overall objective, the Influence Matrix helps in capturing the analytical complexity of the problem to find out what is relevant to the problem and what is not. This can be achieved by asking the right questions. For the barber, who wants to measure the impact of a marketing campaign on the satisfaction of his customers, these questions could be as follows:

To what extent is a marketing campaign able to influence the number of customers?

To what extent is a marketing campaign able to influence the number of visits?

To what extent is a marketing campaign able to influence the rate of customer loss?

What leads to customer loss?

Do the factors that affect customer loss also affect number of visits?

What is a possible marketing campaign to reach customers?

What message is appropriate for a marketing campaign?

By answering these and more questions every important quantifiable element of the Influence Matrix is covered to capture analytical

---

2 Charles F. Kettering (1876-1958), US electrical engineer and inventor.

complexity and to state the precise decision problem. Now it is time to structure the Influence Matrix by using those quantitative elements to get to the heart of the decision problem.

CHAPTER II

The Influence Matrix Helps Define the Quantifiable Elements

To visualize the decision problem it is not enough to decompose the problem into quantifiable elements. They also need to be defined to arrange them graphically. The Influence Matrix helps to define the quantifiable elements of the decision problem by distinguishing between values, scenarios, decisions, and uncertainties.

▓ WHAT ARE VALUES?

A value in an Influence Matrix is the criterion that you want to maximize or minimize. Typical examples for financial values are: return on investment, profit, and cash flow. Non-financial values typically are: image, brand awareness, and social responsibility. For the barber-shop example the criterion that the barber wants to maximize by the marketing campaign is customer satisfaction. In the Influence Matrix the value is visualized using a hexagon.

▓ WHAT ARE SCENARIOS?

A scenario is a certain project, investment or action, which includes a bundle of decisions. There are at least two different scenarios. The first scenario is always the "Current Course & Speed" scenario. This scenario points out what will happen to the value, if no project, investment or action is realized and is therefore also called the "do-nothing scenario". Whereas the second scenario represents a new way of doing business in the form of a new project, investment or another action that influences the value. Having at least two different scenarios offers an opportunity to compare them. Later on, this provides information on which scenario has a more positive effect on the value and therefore is preferable. Of course, it is also possible to include three or more scenarios in an Influence Matrix. Implementing new software systems is a common example, where organizations create one scenario for each software provider, which often leads to the creation of more than five different scenarios.

For the customer satisfaction example there will be two scenarios to make it easier to grasp. The first scenario is "Current Course & Speed", which means that the barber does not improve anything and keeps doing business as usual. The second scenario is the "Marketing Campaign", in which the barber offers his existing and new customers a onetime 20% discount on a haircut on Thursdays between 8-12 a.m. in the newspaper. The barber noticed that he often had to refuse customers due to schedule conflicts. However, every Thursday between 8-12 a.m. he experiences that employees are idle. Additionally, the advertisement offers a new special service, which includes a onetime free head massage. The barber supposes that his lack of service quality has led to a higher customer loss. That is why he thinks starting this marketing campaign enables an increased customer satisfaction. In the Influence Matrix the scenarios are visualized using a rectangle.

<u>Scenarios:</u>

- Current Course & Speed
- Marketing Campaign

■WHAT ARE DECISIONS?

A decision is everything that you are able to control. Typical examples of decisions are project budgets and resources. The decisions the barber is able to control are: how much money he will spend on the marketing campaign, which marketing channel he will use, when he wants the campaign to start and stop, which marketing medium he will use, what his target audience is, what the message of the campaign is, and what offers he makes. In the Influence Matrix decisions are visualized using a rectangle.

Decisions:

- Budget
- Channel
- Timing
- Medium
- Target Audience
- Message
- Offer

■WHAT ARE UNCERTAINTIES?

An uncertainty is everything that you are not able to control. Uncertainties are the heart of every Influence Matrix. They determine the outcome of the value, which needs to be quantified. By asking the questions in chapter I the barber is now able to make the Influence Matrix mutually exclusive and collectively exhaustive by adding all uncertainties he comes across. This so called MECE principle assures that every element in the Influence Matrix is distinct and separate and does not overlap with another element (mutually exclusive) while all elements together represent the complete decision problem (collectively exhaustive). This avoids the problem of double counting of any element as well as the risk of overlooking information.

For the customer satisfaction example uncertainties, which the barber is not able to control, are: current value of the client, potential value of the client, frequency of visits, monetary value per visit, latency between visits, number of visits, number of current customers, number of new customers, and friction, which is basically everything that leads to less visits. In general two kinds of frictions have to be distinguished, emotional friction and physical friction. Emotional friction is everything "soft" that leads to a higher customer loss, such as dissatisfaction due to poor service. Whereas physical friction is more about external circumstances, such as dissatisfaction due to schedule conflicts.[3] In the Influence Matrix uncertainties are visualized using an oval.

Potential
Customer Value

---

3 Novo, 2004, p. 25.

CHAPTER III

The Influence Matrix Relates the Quantifiable Elements

When all relevant elements (value, scenarios, decisions, and uncertainties) of the decision problem are specified and detected, another important task of the Influence Matrix has to be performed. Stating every relevant factor of the decision problem still does not tell you how they are interrelated. A lot of decision-makers are not aware that the relationships between decisions and uncertainties, uncertainties and value, or uncertainty and uncertainty have great impact on the outcome. They rather try to turn a blind eye on the relationship between single Influence Matrix factors, although it is evident that due to ignoring certain relationships, dependencies, and correlations essential information gets lost for further analysis of the decision problem.

INFLUENCES SHOW DEPENDENCIES BETWEEN QUANTIFIABLE ELEMENTS

Influences show relationships, dependencies, and correlations between the different elements of an Influence Matrix. Since every element of the Influence Matrix is based on the state of knowledge of a particular person, influences represent a flow of information. They indicate a causal relationship. Influences are also necessary and relevant for the building of the financial model afterwards. Influences can exist between uncertainties, uncertainties and values, scenarios and decisions, and decision and uncertainties. They are indicated by an arrow.

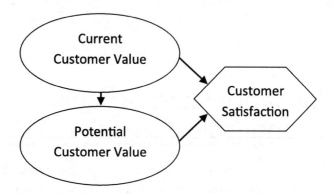

■ RULES FOR CONSTRUCTING AN INFLUENCE MATRIX

Theoretically an Influence Matrix can be expanded to almost infinity. A specific value within an Influence Matrix does not mean that there is no other superior value. However, looking at a project, investment or action the value of the Influence Matrix for that specific project, investment or action needs to be identified and not the superior values, which result from e.g. the organization's mission statement. Another element of the Influence Matrix decision-makers often waste time on is related to the uncertainties and can be called "the over decomposition problem". We often observe that decision-makers get lost in the details of an uncertainty. If the costs of a project, investment or action are for example a minor uncertainty it is sufficient to only state one "cost" oval as an uncertainty. If a huge difference in uncertainty between fixed and variable costs can be distinguished, even two ovals with "fixed costs" and "variable costs" can be included in the Influence Matrix. However, to split up the uncertainty of cost into every cost factor involved in the project, investment or action would not result in an additional benefit in most cases, when a total cost price can be estimated easier.

Therefore, the size of the Influence Matrix heavily depends on the problem definition you stated earlier. When a level of detail in the Influence Matrix is reached, where intuition and judgment can be used to make meaningful assessments, no more input for the Influence Matrix is needed and additions to the Influence Matrix have to be stopped.

To construct a meaningful Influence Matrix, two simple rules have to be obeyed:

1. No Loops

Since the arrows in the Influence Matrix represent a flow of information, it is not possible that following a path in the Influence Matrix leads back to where started.

2. No forgetting previously known information

If an arrow indicates a relationship between two elements all subsequent elements are also affected by this relationship. One of the main objectives and advantages of the Influence Matrix is to visualize the decision problem on just a single sheet of paper. Due to the fact that a lot of decision problems are highly complex a tangled mass of uncertainties can arise. To maintain clarity in the Influence Matrix it is possible to group uncertainties, which results in less distracting influence arrows and more available space. Due to this technique the Influence Matrix can be neatly arranged without any loss of information. The only thing that needs to be kept in mind is that the newly built group of uncertainties has the same measurement as well as the same incoming and outgoing influence arrows. If not, essential information and dependencies get lost.

■CUSTOMER SATISFACTION INFLUENCE MATRIX AND HOW TO HANDLE IT

Knowing how an Influence Matrix has to be built and how it works enables the barber from the practical example to build his own Influence Matrix for his specific customer satisfaction problem. For other practical examples of Influence Matrices see Appendix I. Bearing the rules and advice on how to construct an Influence Matrix in mind the barber's Influence Matrix looks as follows:

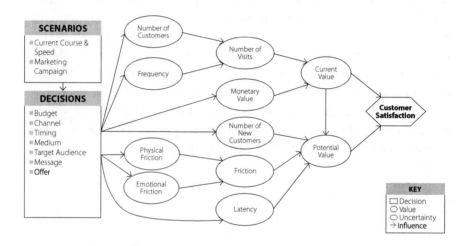

Figure 1 – The Influence Matrix displays elements of the decision problem

As described earlier in chapter II the chosen scenarios are "Current Course & Speed" and "Marketing Campaign". Resulting from the scenarios the barber is able to deduce decisions, which in this case are: budget for the marketing campaign, the chosen marketing channel, the timing of the marketing campaign, the used medium, the identified target audience, the chosen marketing message, and the actual offer. These are all factors the barber is able to control and decide on in contrast to the uncertainties. Those are the elements of the Influence Matrix the barber is not able to control. The uncertainties, which are influenced by the decisions, are: physical and emotional friction, latency between visits, number of customers, frequency of visits, number of visits, monetary value of visits, number of new customers, and current and potential value of his customers. In the end, all these uncertainties join in the value of customer satisfaction. Normally one would say that customer satisfaction is the cause for a change in number of customers, frequency, physical friction etc. However, in the Influence Matrix the cause-result relationship is illustrated the other way around. Because customer satisfaction is not observable for the barber, he needs factors with which he is able to measure customer satisfaction. Therefore, he needs these observable factors, which are the uncertainties in the Influence Matrix. The arrows from the left to the right represent that customer satisfaction can be determined by using observable and measurable indicators such as number of customers, frequency, etc.

The first hurdle on the path to the quantification of qualitative values is overcome by having built the Influence Matrix for the decision problem. The next step to take is building the financial model based on the Influence Matrix to establish the basis for the sensitivity analysis.

PART II

The Financial Model Quantifies the Elements of the Influence Matrix

Using the given information in the Influence Matrix, it is now time to make use of the second tool on the path to the quantification of qualitative values: the financial model. There are many definitions of what a financial model is, what it is used for, and what it does. We chose the following definition to illustrate that this book is not going to perform magic, but rather uses simple tools to reach the goal of quantifying qualitative values in monetary terms: A financial model is anything that is used to calculate, forecast or estimate financial numbers.

Using Microsoft Excel© a financial model will be created in a spreadsheet. With the financial model every relevant factor for the solution of the decision problem can be covered and the decision processes emulated. Furthermore, the financial model enables you to quantify all elements of the decision-making process to get your budget approved. By using the Influence Matrix as a basis, you are able to quantify every factor relevant to its specific decision problem.

Bearing in mind what an Influence Matrix does, how it works, and how it has to be built it is time to take a look at how it can be used while on the path to the quantification of qualitative values. As described in the introduction, the Influence Matrix is only the first step to reach the goal of quantifying qualitative values. The second step is building the financial model. The Influence Matrix enables you to structure the financial model by using its values, scenarios, decisions, uncertainties, and of course their dependencies.

CHAPTER IV

How to Create the Structure of the Financial Model

Formulating a financial model in a structured way is important for three reasons. First of all, structuring the financial model helps you to have a better overview of the model. This enables you to work more efficient, productive, and effective on the models' content and also provides a better overview of already included and still missing information. Second, a good structure reduces the margin of error. Given that errors are inevitable, some structuring techniques are more prone to error than others. Therefore, choosing the right technique will reduce errors, as well as audit and review time. Third, a well structured financial model assists others in quickly grasping the concept of the model, which reduces the amount of time normally needed for explanation.

The structure of a financial model depends to a great extent on its purpose and use. This means that there is no standard layout or design, which can be used for every financial model constructed. However, there are guidelines used to create at least good practice, which enable reduction of error, audit time, and help users and readers to comprehend the financial model more easily.

There are two main approaches, which can be used to structure a financial model: the top-down approach and the bottom-up approach. While the top-down approach identifies the purpose or objective of your model, followed by the consideration of the usage of the model, the bottom-up approach prioritizes the collection and input of the raw data. From a methodical work point of view, it is helpful to work with the top-down approach to build a financial model. This approach includes the user's involvement from the outset and focuses more on the outcome and purpose of your model. Thus working from the top down enables you to manage your expectations easier and in doing so clarify the modeling task.

Since the Influence Matrix created earlier already points out the purpose of the model and includes every relevant factor of the decision problem, it is undeniable that it is useful to structure the financial model top-down. Reflecting on the Influence Matrix, the barber can use the decisions, uncertainties, and the value to give his financial model the appropriate structure. As the purpose of the barber's financial model is to calculate the effect of the scenarios (Current Course & Speed and Marketing Campaign) on his value (customer satisfaction), this enables him to state the outcome of his model, which is the comparison of the two scenarios with respect to the customer satisfaction in the form of a cash flow.

Additionally, the barber is able to arrange the decisions and uncertainties that influence customer satisfaction, giving the financial model its structure. As seen in chapter III customer satisfaction derives from the uncertainties current value and potential value, which on their part depend on other uncertainties. This provides the barber with the information he needs to structure the following financial model:

	A	B
8	**Current value**	Number of customers (per year)
9		Frequency (per year)
10		Number of visits (per year)
11		Monetary value (per visit)
12		Current value (per year)
13		
14	**Potential value**	Physical friction due to scheduling conflicts (% of customers)
15		Emotional friction due to poor service (% of customers)
16		Number of new customers due to marketing campaign
17		Number of potential customers (per year)
18		Current latency (in days)
19		Latency due to friction (in days)
20		Frequency due to friction
21		Number of potential visits (per year)
22		Monetary value (per visit)
23		Potential value (per year)
24		
25	**Customer satisfaction**	Loss due to friction
26		Costs of marketing campaign
27		
28		Net cash flow
29		Net cash flow (scenarios compared)

Figure 2 – The financial model is based on the Influence Matrix

▓ KEEP THE FINANCIAL MODEL SIMPLE

The simplicity of a financial model has a bigger influence on mistakes and errors than its structure. When a problem arises a modeler only has his mental map when trying to figure out what is wrong with the model. Unfortunately a problem in a specific area of the model does not compulsively mean that the cause for that problem lies in anything, which seems to be related to it, e.g. a formula. As a result you should keep in mind that the more things can be done correctly the first time around, the less trouble and confusion is caused.

Doing things more correctly the first time can be achieved by paying attention to one key principle of financial modeling: keep the financial model simple. This does not mean that your model should be minimized to its most ordinary form and do nothing but the most rudimentary of calculations. It rather means that the best solution is almost always the simplest one to come by. Therefore, you should keep formulas simple even if this means using more than one line to break a calculation. Additionally, you should keep the structure of the model simple with a flow of calculations that goes in one consistent direction, preferably from the beginning to the end. Furthermore, you should keep formatting simple with just enough to make visual distinctions on the screen to help the people reading your financial model. Bold type is helpful for highlighting items. However, if the spreadsheet holds a profusion of bold types then the highlighting effect is gone.

■ FINANCIAL MODEL AND INFLUENCE MATRIX NEED TO BE CONGRUENT

When constructing an Influence Matrix you already made sure that the complete decision problem is visualized and every factor involved in the decision process is considered. However, not only the financial model benefits from the input of the Influence Matrix. The Influence Matrix also benefits from the creation of the financial model.

When creating the financial model, it is not unusual that you come across a calculation or formula for which you need additional information or important factors not given or stated in the Influence Matrix. That is why often during the process of creating a financial model important factors concerning the decision problem are revealed, which leads to an even more precise definition of the problem and an adjustment of the Influence Matrix. Thus, financial model and Influence Matrix form a symbiotic relationship since they complement each other. The ability of these two tools to cross check one another is also the reason why in the end Influence Matrix and financial model always need to be congruent. If they are not congruent, the Influence Matrix is either missing a relevant scenario, decision, uncertainty, or value or the financial model is missing an important element, which needs to be considered within the calculations.

When the financial model is in sync with the Influence Matrix, you are able to move forward to the next step in creating the financial model: convert all dependent factors within the Influence Matrix into formulas.

CHAPTER V

How to Convert Dependencies into Formulas

The Influence Matrix does not only assist you when structuring the financial model. It also provides you with dependencies and relationships of all elements involved in the decision problem. This gives you direct insight on which cells of your spreadsheet model need to be interlinked. Your task is to decide to what extent they are related.

Microsoft Excel© offers a wide range of formulas to perform calculations. Fortunately, knowing the simplest formulas Microsoft Excel© offers is sufficient to quantify qualitative values in monetary terms. Almost every financial model can be built on four basic arithmetic operations or the combination of them to perform the most important calculations: Addition, subtraction, multiplication, and division (if you are already familiar with Microsoft Excel©, you can skip the following 2 paragraphs). In Microsoft Excel© these calculations are constructed as follows:

◢	A	B	C	D	E
1		Digit 1	Digit 2	Result	
2	Addition	3	4	7	<-- =B2+C2
3					
4	Subtraction	8	6	2	<-- =B4-C4
5					
6	Multiplication	5	2	10	<-- =B6*C6
7					
8	Division	9	3	3	<-- =B8/C8

Figure 3 – The arithmetic calculations are the basis to build a financial model

In Microsoft Excel© every formula is introduced by starting with the "=" sign. Addends are summed up by using the "+" sign, subtrahends are subtracted by using the "-" sign, factors are multiplied using the "*" sign, and divisors are divided by using the "/" sign.

When combining these formulas, you need to consider the BODMAS principle. BODMAS stands for: Brackets, order, division, multiplication, addition, and subtraction; and is the principle of arithmetic priority. When =1+2*3 is calculated in Microsoft Excel© the result is 7, while =(1+2)*3 equals 9. The BODMAS principle simply states that brackets around each calculation help to avoid errors.

Error elimination is also an important topic, when talking about converting dependencies into formulas. When performing calculations and especially combining formulas, we often observed that formulas from project groups end up in a bewildering length and complexity. Keeping chapter IV in mind, the utilized formulas need to be kept simple. For example formulas running on over four lines require considerable time and effort for others to understand and they are difficult to audit and review. Instead of using four line formulas you should rather split the calculation into various cells and decompose it. Additionally, the longer a formula gets the more it is prone to error. Although every modeler experiences the greatest satisfaction when a four line formula actually works, it is one of the biggest sources of error in the whole financial model. Furthermore, what a financial model tries to achieve is to create confidence in its results, however if the reviewer is unable to understand a formula, we are failing to give him the confidence he needs to rely on the results of your model.

The barber strives to consider all these factors and starts to convert every dependency present in the Influence Matrix into formulas. He immediately notices that the structure he previously constructed is very helpful. However, to have an even better overview of the dependencies of the factors the barber uses another technique: he names certain cells. To name a cell has a crucial advantage. When reviewing or auditing a financial model it is sometimes hard to follow every formula. This makes it a tough challenge when figuring out which cell a formula is referring to. By giving names to the cells, the dependencies included within the formula can directly be seen and do not require additional time consuming cell hunt through the whole spreadsheet. So instead of e.g. performing the calculation for a cell, which contains the profit formula "=A8-K49" the cells A8 and K49 are named as "Benefits" and "Costs". As a result, the new formula for profit is "=Benefits-Costs", which clearly states which cells are used and to what extent they are related.

After naming the most important cells of his financial model, which is comparable to defining variables in programming, the barber continues converting the dependencies present in the Influence Matrix into formulas. The current value part of the customer satisfaction financial model should be built as follows:

	A	B	C	D	E	F	G	H
8	Current value	Number of customers (per year)	0	<-- CCandS_Number_of_customers				
9		Frequency (per year)	0	<-- CCandS_Frequency				
10		Number of visits (per year)	0	<-- =CCandS_Number_of_customers*CCandS_Frequency				
11		Monetary value (per visit)	- €	<-- CCandS_Monetary_value				
12		Current value (per year)	- €	<-- =CCandS_Number_of_visits*CCandS_Monetary_value				

Figure 4 – The relationship between the elements is converted into formulas

The cells in column C are named according to what they imply. C8 for example is named CCandS_Number_of_customers, which stands for the number of customers in the current course and speed scenario (the marketing campaign scenario will be added later). The number of visits per year is calculated by the number of customers per year multiplied by the average frequency per year. This is why the formula in cell C10 for the number of visits is =CCandS_Number_of_customers *CCandS_Frequency. Without naming the cells the formula for number of visits per year would be =C8*C9. This would induce further research in the spreadsheet about where and what these cells are. By naming the cells the relationship and dependency can directly be seen and immediately understood.

After structuring the financial model and converting dependencies present in the Influence Matrix into formulas it is time to insert the data for every specific cell. However, the collection of data is also an important step and therefore needs special attention.

CHAPTER VI
How to Collect Data by Interviewing Subject Matter Experts

To complete the financial model, the only thing missing is the actual data input. Of course every modeler is able to fill in the data himself, which is the case for the barber in the practical example. However, when undertaking projects with a larger scale the modeler would struggle filling in relevant data, which he simply does not know. Here the GIGO principle takes effect. GIGO stands for Garbage In, Garbage Out. This principle was originally applied to computer software meaning that if invalid data is entered into a system, the resulting output will also be invalid. No matter how well the financial model is constructed, the GIGO principle expresses clearly that inserting wrong or uncertain data will result in wrong or at least unreliable outcomes of the financial model.

Because the quality of the results heavily depends on the data input, it is of great importance that only people who are qualified to make profound statements provide the data for filling in the cells. That is why collecting data for the financial model is carried out by interviewing subject matter experts. The Influence Matrix provides you with information on who is to be interviewed in order to collect the specific data. If for example the weighted average cost of capital is considered an uncertainty in your project, the Chief Financial Officer needs to be asked. If within the same project the amount of sold products is an uncertainty, your sales director needs to be interviewed. This way, all needed data for the financial model is collected by interviewing the employees according to their special field of work.

Theoretically interviewing subject matter experts sounds like the best approach when creating a profound financial model. In practice, however, many organizations refuse to accept this simple method for one reason: time. They argue that the employees, who need to be interviewed, are very important employees and have much more important tasks to perform than being interviewed. People arguing in this way unfortunately ignore the GIGO principle. Wrong or uncertain data provided by someone who is not an expert in the field of work can lead to fatal losses within a project.

Not long ago we worked on a project for an insurance company, which was about the implementation of a new business intelligence solution. To create the appropriate Business Case we needed to interview the employee who was responsible for the distribution of all reports. Unfortunately this employee said that he would not have time to have a little chat with us. At the end of the project the Business Case Analysis resulted in a positive cash flow with a certainty of 80%. However, the risk analysis stated that the success of the project depends to 90% on the information about the reports and that this information has a monetary impact of 1,800,000 €. Normally a subject matter expert interview does not take longer than half an hour. The question is: is sacrificing half an hour for an interview worse for an organization than spending thousands or even millions of Euro in a hopeless project, because someone did not have 30 minutes for an interview? It is not!

■ WHY APPROXIMATELY RIGHT BEATS PRECISELY WRONG

Another issue, which occurs during many interviews, is the problem of the interviewee to provide you with precise data. "How am I supposed to know the exact number of that?" or "I simply do not know how much it exactly is!" are frequent answers during subject matter expert interviews. However that is no problem at all. The goal of quantifying qualitative values is to forecast to what extent a scenario will have a positive or negative impact on your value. This means the analysis you are going to undertake predicts future results and therefore you have to base your results on assumptions. So if anyone is going to say "Your analysis is nothing but assumptions!" you can reply "That is absolutely right!". Since nobody is able to make a precise estimate about numbers, which refer to the future and therefore are more or less uncertain, it is appropriate to work with ranges. So instead of stating only one number for an assumption, it is more accurate to state a range of three numbers for an assumption, namely a minimum-, most likely-, and maximum value. During the subject matter expert interviews, the interviewee is no longer asked to state only one specific number, but rather what he thinks is the absolute minimum-, most likely-, and maximum value.

Imagine your Chief Financial Officer (CFO) is asked to forecast the exchange rate of the US dollar to the Euro for the next year. Of course he could state only one single number e.g. $1.56. But how likely is it that this number is 100% correct? If he instead states a minimum value of $1.31, a most likely value of $1.52, and a maximum value of $1.75 the probability is higher that the exchange rate for the next year will be in the range of these values. Therefore it is better to be approximately right than to be precisely wrong.

Working with a minimum-, most likely-, and maximum value provides you with the certainty that the exact number lies somewhere in between the given values. Using ranges also facilitates the data ascertainment for the interviewee and prevents statements such as "How am I supposed to know the exact number?" or "I simply do not know how much it exactly is!". Instead of being compelled to provide you with only one number, the interviewee is able to state a range. Therefore he is not pressured to know the exact number. However, even if it is better to be approximately right using ranges instead of being precisely wrong using point estimates, a smaller range is of course more precise than a wider range. Therefore it is helpful to calibrate the assumptions of subject matter experts.

▪CALIBRATE THE ASSUMPTIONS OF SUBJECT MATTER EXPERTS

Calibrating the assumptions of subject matter experts is important for one crucial reason: the more accurate the assumptions, the more reliable the result. Since the results of the financial model are based on assumptions made by subject matter experts, the reliability of the results depends on the quality of the given assumptions.

To improve the quality of the assumptions, you need to reduce the uncertainty concerning the given information during the subject matter expert interviews. The uncertainty can be reduced by using a method, which expresses uncertainty about a number by thinking of it as a range of probable values. In statistics, a range that has a particular chance of containing the correct answer is called a confidence interval (CI).

To clarify what a CI is, here is an example: a 90% CI is a range that has a 90% chance of containing the correct answer. For example no sales manager can possibly know for certain exactly how many of his current prospects will turn into customers in the next quarter. However, the sales manager thinks that probably no less than 3 prospects and probably no more than 7 prospects will sign contracts. If he is 90% sure the actual number will fall between 3 and 7, then it can be said that there is a 90% CI of 3 to 7. Using a CI of 90% during the subject matter expert interviews leads to better data input since major outlier assumptions are avoided and uncertainty is reduced by preventing the interviewees from swerving away from crucial data.

■ COMPLETE THE FINANCIAL MODEL BY ADDING DATA

After creating the model structure, converting dependencies into formulas, and knowing how to collect data by interviewing subject matter experts, you are now able to complete the financial model by adding data. While working on a project with a larger scale there are knowledgeable experts about every uncertainty within the Influence Matrix. The barber from the example case is the expert for every uncertainty of his model. Every cell, which has been left blank, now needs to be filled with his information within a 90% confidence interval. Since the barber has already added the dependencies and relationships of the different elements of the decision problem he only needs to add his data to the model, while Microsoft Excel© automatically generates the result. The data he needs to add in order to complete the financial model are the minimum-, most likely-, and maximum values of: Number of customers, Frequency, Monetary value, Physical friction, Emotional friction, Number of new customers, Latency, and Costs of marketing campaign.

For a better visual overview of which cells are data entries and which are not, it is advantageous to mark them with colors. In the barber case he marked the data entry cells blue, while the derived results are marked yellow. After adding the data to the financial model, the financial model looks as follows:

		Current Course & Speed Scenario			Marketing Campaign Scenario		
		Minimum	Most Likely	Maximum	Minimum	Most Likely	Maximum
Key							
	Blue: Data Entry						
	Yellow: Derived Results						
Current value	Number of customers (per year)	400	450	500	400	450	500
	Frequency (per year)	7	9	11	7	9	11
	Number of visits (per year)	2800	4050	5500	2800	4050	5500
	Monetary value (per visit)	23 €	25 €	27 €	23 €	25 €	27 €
	Current value (per year)	64.400 €	101.250 €	148.500 €	64.400 €	101.250 €	148.500 €
Potential value	Physical friction due to scheduling conflicts (% of customers)	15%	20%	25%	5%	10%	15%
	Emotional friction due to poor service (% of customers)	7%	10%	13%	5%	8%	11%
	Number of new customers due to marketing campaign	0	0	0	80	90	100
	Number of potential customers (per year)	312	315	310	440	459	470
	Current latency (in days)	52	41	33	52	41	33
	Latency due to friction (in days)	60	45	35	55	40	30
	Frequency due to friction	6	8	10	7	9	12
	Number of potential visits (per year)	1898	2555	3233	2920	4188	5718
	Monetary value (per visit)	23 €	25 €	27 €	23 €	25 €	27 €
	Potential value (per year)	43.654 €	63.875 €	87.287 €	67.160 €	104.705 €	154.395 €
Customer satisfaction	Loss due to friction	- 20.746 €	- 37.375 €	- 61.213 €	2.760 €	3.459 €	5.895 €
	Costs of marketing campaign	- €	- €	- €	10.000 €	10.000 €	10.000 €
	Net cash flow	- 20.746 €	- 37.375 €	- 61.213 €	7.240 €	6.541 €	4.105 €
	Net cash flow (scenarios compared)	- €	- €	- €	13.506 €	30.834 €	57.108 €

Figure 5 – The financial model illustrates the quantification

With reference to the most likely values, the barber assumes that during the next year he will lose 20% of his customers due to the current scheduling conflicts. Additionally, he assumes that he will lose another 10% due to poor service. For the Current Course & Speed scenario this friction would result in a potential value of only 63,875 €, which is an overall loss of 37,375 € compared to the current value of 101,250 €. In other words, the net cash flow will decrease by 37,375 € due to less customer satisfaction.

Taking a look at the Marketing Campaign scenario the barber assumes he can reduce the physical friction by 10% and the emotional friction by 2%. Additionally, the barber expects to gain 90 new customers due to the marketing campaign and a latency of only 40 days. These assumptions for the Marketing Campaign scenario lead to a plus of 3,459 €. However, in the Marketing Campaign scenario the barber also has to consider the marketing cost, which is 10,000 € and results in a loss of 6,541 €. After analyzing the cash flow results, the barber compares the two scenarios. He instantly recognizes that the loss would be much greater if he does not change something and continues with the Current Course & Speed scenario. In the most likely case, the loss would be reduced by 30,834 € if he starts the new marketing campaign.

Comparing the two scenarios, the quintessence of the cash flow analysis is that increasing the customers' satisfaction due to the marketing campaign has a monetary value of 13,506 € in the minimum-, 30,834 € in the most likely, and 57,108 € in the maximum case. But how probable are these outcomes and what are the biggest risk factors? To answer these questions the barber performs a sensitivity analysis as explained in the following chapter.

PART III

The Sensitivity Analysis Provides Certainty and Identifies the Risk Factors

We often hear of Business Cases with conclusions such as "Undertaking this investment will result in increased revenue of 1,594,823 € over 3 years". Of course the audience of the Business Case presentation will ask: "How probable is this number and what are the risk factors?". We bet that in 99.9% of all Business Cases made, the exact result of the calculation will never be reached. But that is no problem at all. To get more certainty about the result and to identify the risk factors we make use of the sensitivity analysis.

In general, sensitivity analysis can be applied in a broad range of fields. It can be used to determine a model's resemblance with the process under study, the quality of a model definition or the factors that contribute most to the output variability. Additionally, it can be used to determine the region in the space of input factors for which a model variation is maximum, the optimal - or instability - regions within the space of factors for use in a subsequent calibration study, or interactions between factors. Sensitivity analysis is popular in financial applications, risk analysis, signal processing, neural networks and any area where models are developed, because it provides certainty with the results.

For this book sensitivity analysis is the study of how the variation (uncertainty) in the output of a mathematical model can be apportioned, qualitatively or quantitatively, to different sources of variation in the input of the model.

This is what the next part will cover and what you need to know. The most frequent questions participants ask us during our public seminars *www.business-case-seminar.com*, because of their accountability towards others, are: "How certain are my results?", "What are the biggest risk factors within my project?", "What is the probability of a negative cash flow?", or "To what extent does the risk take effect on my cash flow results?". As the definition implies, the sensitivity analysis will enable you to take a look at how the uncertainties in the output of the financial model are assigned to the different inputs. Therefore, all these questions can be answered by applying sensitivity analysis to the financial model.

Many areas of application of sensitivity analysis require a high level of statistical understanding. However, this section of the book will concentrate more on how these statistics can provide you with useful information than explaining how these statistics work in detail. Therefore not every method of sensitivity analysis will be explained, but rather the two most important ones you need to quantify qualitative values in monetary terms. These two methods are the Monte Carlo simulation, which determines the probability of outcomes and the tornado diagram, which determines underlying risk factors.

CHAPTER VII

Use Monte Carlo Simulation for Probabilistic Outcomes

By applying sensitivity analysis to the financial model you are able to uncover the likelihood of your results. We often experience that many organizations today simply say that there is a "high", "medium", or "low" chance of reaching a specific goal. However, terms like these do not have a specific monetary value. This is why nobody in such organizations would be able to state whether a medium-risk investment with a 15% return on investment would be better or worse than a high-risk investment with a 50% return on investment. As already discussed in chapter VI, using ranges to represent uncertainty instead of unrealistically precise point estimates clearly has advantages. Whenever an individual uses ranges and probabilities, he or she does not really have to assume anything that is not known for a fact. However, precise estimates have the advantage of being simple to add, subtract, multiply, and divide in a spreadsheet. So how do you add, subtract, multiply, and divide in a spreadsheet when you only have ranges and no exact estimates? Fortunately, a fairly simple method can be done on any PC. This method is the Monte Carlo simulation.

A Monte Carlo simulation uses a computer to generate a large number of trials based on probabilities of the inputs. For each trial, a specific value is randomly generated for each of the uncertain variables. Then these specific values are put into a formula to compute an output for that single trial. This process is repeated for thousands of trials. In other words, it calculates numerous trials of a model by repeatedly picking values from a probability distribution for the uncertain variables. Commonly, a simulation calculates hundreds or thousands of trials in just a few seconds. The value used for each uncertain variable for each trial is selected randomly from the defined possibilities.

Fortunately, you do not have to build Monte Carlo simulations from scratch these days. One tool which you can use instead of writing your own macros is Crystal Ball© from Oracle© (for a 140 days free trial version of Crystal Ball© see Appendix III). Crystal Ball© is a user friendly Microsoft Excel© plug-in, which uses Monte Carlo simulation to calculate probabilistic outcomes and thus takes the uncertainty out of decision-making so you can get your budget approved.

However, Crystal Ball© is not the only program on the market, which provides you with Monte Carlo simulations. Other software programs from SAS or @Risk from Palisade serve the same purpose. In this book however, we make use of Crystal Ball© because of its convenient graphical user interface.

■DEFINE AN ASSUMPTION WITH SIMULATION SOFTWARE

To run a Monte Carlo simulation the uncertain variables mentioned earlier need to be defined. In Crystal Ball© these uncertain variables are called assumptions. They are entered and stored in assumption cells. Assumption cells contain the values that you are unsure of: the uncertain variables in the problem you are trying to solve. The assumption cells must contain simple numeric values, not formulas or text. For each uncertain variable in a simulation, or assumption, you define the possible values with a probability distribution. The type of distribution selected depends on the underlying phenomenon. The most common distribution types are normal-, triangular, uniform-, and lognormal distribution.

Normal   Triangular   Uniform   Lognormal

Figure 6 – The four most common distributions

The normal distribution usually describes many natural phenomena such as IQs, people's heights, the inflation rate, or errors in measurements. The triangular distribution is commonly used when the minimum, most likely, and maximum are known. In the uniform distribution, all values between the minimum and maximum are equally likely to occur. The lognormal distribution is widely used in situations where values are positively skewed (where most of the values occur near the minimum value) such as in financial analysis for stock prices or in real estate for property valuation. For more information about these four distributions see Appendix II.

After defining the input (assumptions) of the financial model, the output needs to be defined, which in Crystal Ball© terms is called defining a "forecast". Since every trial produces associated results, Crystal Ball© also keeps track of the forecasts for each trial. These are important outputs of the model, such as cash flow. They are defined with formulas in spreadsheet forecast cells. For each forecast, Crystal Ball© recalls the cell value for all the trials. In the case of the barber discussed earlier, it will now be explained how defining assumptions and forecasts in Crystal Ball© is done practically.

To run the Monte Carlo simulations it is the barber's task to define the assumptions and the forecast. As explained above, the assumption cells are the uncertain variables, which in the barber's financial model are basically all blue cells, since they represent the data entries (e.g. Number of customers).

◢	A	B	C	D	E
6			Current Course & Speed Scenario		
7			Minimum	Most Likely	Maximum
8	Current value	Number of customers (per year)	400	450	500

Figure 7 – The element "Number of customers" is an example for a data entry

He now has to follow four simple steps when defining the assumption "Number of customers":

1) Select cell D8, then click on Crystal Ball's© *Cell -> Define Assumption*

2) Chose a distribution from the Crystal Ball's© distribution list
In this case, the barber chooses for the triangular distribution, since he knows the minimum-, maximum-, and most likely value. He moves on to the next step:

3) Enter uncertain variables and a name for the assumption

In the array "name" the barber needs to fill in the name of the assumption, which is important for the further analysis he is going to perform. In the arrays "Minimum", "Likeliest", and "Maximum" the barber fills in the suggestions he has about the minimum-, most likely- and maximum number of customers. In order to do so, he uses a convenient Crystal Ball© function, which creates a dynamic cell reference to D8. This means, whenever the barber changes the data entry for cell D8, Crystal Ball© will automatically apply the new data entry for its Monte Carlo simulation, too. Then he moves to the last step:

4) Click *Enter* to see the depiction of the defined distribution and press *OK* to return to the spreadsheet

The Crystal Ball© window, in which the barber defines the assumption, looks as follows:

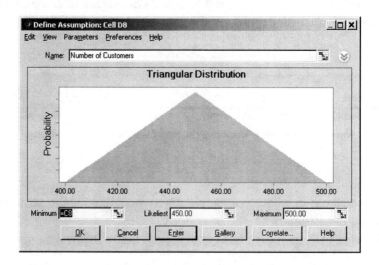

Figure 8 – For every data entry an assumption needs to be defined

Normally it does not take longer than a few seconds to define an assumption with Crystal Ball©. The barber now has to define all other blue data entries as assumptions. Because he will use the triangular distribution for each assumption, he is able to use the Crystal Ball© *copy and paste* function, which enables him to define every assumption within his financial model in a few seconds. After doing so, the only thing left to do before running the simulation is to define the forecast.

Defining a forecast with Crystal Ball© is as easy as defining assumptions. The barber only has to select the outcome he wants to forecast. In his case this is the "Net Cash Flow (Scenarios compared)" of his customer satisfaction model. After selecting the cell, the following window pops up:

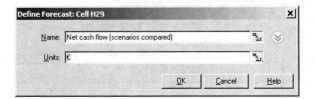

Figure 9 – The outcome needs to be defined as a forecast

The barber only has to enter the name of his forecast "Net cash flow (scenarios compared)" and the units it should be expressed in (€). Theoretically the barber could define different forecasts, for example the net cash flow of his Current Course & Speed scenario or the net cash flow of his Marketing Campaign scenario. However, what interests him most is of course the comparison of both his scenarios. The comparison between these two net cash flows will namely provide him with the information on what the monetary benefit of the new marketing campaign is compared to doing nothing (Current Course & Speed scenario).

■ANALYZE THE PROBABILITY DENSITY FUNCTION

To run the Monte Carlo simulation the barber simply needs to press *Run* in the Crystal Ball© options. After a few seconds, which Crystal Ball© needs to run the entered number of trials (in this case 100.000), the probability density function for the forecasted value appears automatically and is as follows:

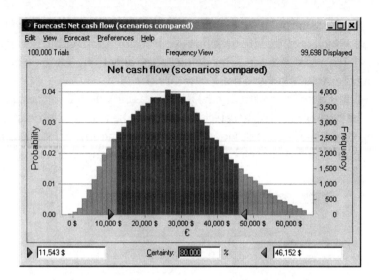

Figure 10 – The probability density function shows the probability of the result

The graph is divided into several intervals (blue and red columns). The height of every column represents how many times during the 100,000 trials the value on the x-axis occurred (frequency). The highest column for example occurred about 4,000 times during the 100,000 trials and has a monetary value of about 23,000 €. During our seminars *www.business-case-seminar.com* we made hundreds of evaluations with the result that in most cases the audience of the Business Case presentation either wants to see the probability of breaking even or the certainty of reaching a specific result. With the information given above, you can read off how likely your outcomes are and provide your audience with everything it wishes.

The barber also wants to find out about the likelihood of his outcome. He fills in the percentage of certainty he wants to derive and Crystal Ball© answers him by stating the related monetary values. In figure 10 the barber wanted to know the outcome of the net cash flow with an 80% certainty. The graph has to be read as follows: there is an 80% chance of reaching a positive cash flow between 11,543 € and 46,152 €. As can be seen in figure 10 there is also a low probability that the net cash flow will be negative, since the x-axis reaches into negative values as well. To uncover the percentage at which his net cash flow reaches 0 € he simply drags the triangle within the graph to 0 € and reads off the probability of its outcome.

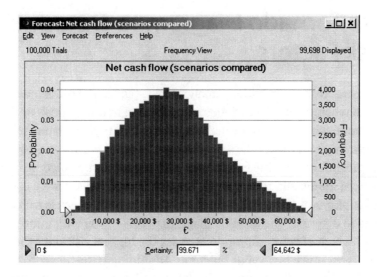

Figure 11 – The probability density function indicates breakeven point

Based on the assumptions the barber made, there is a 99.671% certainty that the new marketing campaign compared to the Current Course & Speed scenario will deliver a monetary value between 0 € and 64,642 €. In other words, the barber does not have to be a risk taker to decide in favor of the new marketing campaign, since there is almost a 100% chance of reaching a positive cash flow.

The barber is completely overwhelmed by the results. He had a gut feeling that the new marketing campaign would have a positive effect on the satisfaction on his customers. However, he did not expect that the analysis would result in such a high certainty of net cash flow being between 0 € and almost 65,000 €. Now that the barber knows how likely his outcomes are and that it is possible to quantify customer satisfaction, there is only one last question he asks himself after running the Monte Carlo simulation: "I can clearly see how certain my results are, but what are the risk factors within my project and to what extent do they have an impact on my results?"

CHAPTER VIII
Use Tornado Diagram to Determine Risk Factors

In general terms a sensitivity analysis investigates the robustness of a model when the model includes some form of mathematical- or financial modeling. A sensitivity analysis tries to identify which uncertainties weight more on the model's conclusions. In other words, sensitivity analysis determines possible risk factors with regard to the outcome of the financial model and their specific impact. Crystal Ball© uses a convenient tool to pinpoint these risk factors and their impact, which is called the tornado diagram. The tornado diagram provides you with information about which of your assumptions poses the biggest risk since they have the largest impacts on your outcome. Additionally, the tornado diagram points out to what extent these risk factors have a monetary impact on your outcome.

The tornado diagram measures the impact of each assumption on the target forecast one at a time. The tool tests each assumption or cell independently. While analyzing one assumption, the tool freezes every other assumption at their most likely values. This measures the effect of each assumption on the forecast cell while removing the effects of the other assumptions. This method is also known as "one-at-a-time perturbation" or "parametric analyses".

■ HOW TO IDENTIFY AND ANALYZE CRUCIAL RISK FACTORS

The barber is still amazed by the amount of money his new marketing campaign could generate due to an increase in customers' satisfaction. However, he wonders what factors are the biggest risk factors of his project and to what extent these factors influence his net cash flow. To find out about this, he runs the tornado tool, which is integrated in the Crystal Ball© software. To run the tornado tool the barber only needs to use the assumptions and the forecasts, which he already did as described in chapter VII. After that he just needs to make use of the Crystal Ball© tool bar, select the tornado diagram option and run the tornado diagram by selecting the forecast (Net cash flow scenarios compared), adding the assumptions and then leaving the rest to the default options. Doing so, Crystal Ball© provides the barber with the following tornado diagram:

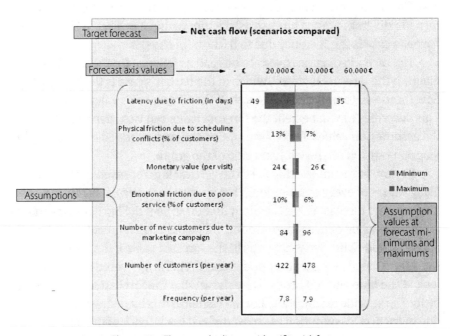

Figure 12 – The tornado diagram identifies risk factors

The tornado diagram tool tests the range of each assumption at percentiles and then calculates the value of the forecast at each point. The tornado diagram illustrates the swing between the maximum and minimum forecast values for each assumption. The variable that causes the largest swing appears at the top and the variable that causes the smallest swing appears at the bottom. The upper assumptions have the most effect on the forecast and the lower assumptions have the least effect on the forecast. This is the reason why the assumptions which appear at the top of the tornado diagram are the biggest risk factors within a project, which in the barber's case is the "Latency due to friction (in days)".

The tornado diagram needs to be read as follows: On the top of the diagram the forecast is stated, which in the barber's case is the "Net cash flow (scenarios compared)". Beneath it, the forecast axis values are listed. This describes to what extent the forecast value can vary, depending on the assumption values. Every assumption the barber added to the tornado diagram is listed on the left hand side of the graph.

So now to the interesting part, the vertical line represents the most likely values of every assumption. That is why the vertical line hits the axis with the forecast values at about 30,000 €. So if the barber takes the most likely value of every assumption, this would deliver a net cash flow of about 30,000 €. But what happens to the forecast value if the minimum or maximum value of the assumption is used? This is answered by taking a look at the blue and red boxes. They show what the forecasted value would be for the specific assumption. Let me visualize this by taking the "Latency due to friction" assumption as an example. If the latency of the barber's customers is an average of 49 days, this would have a negative impact on the forecasted value. The net cash flow would be reduced by approximately 10,000 €, while other assumptions are frozen and not taken into consideration. However, if the latency of the barber's customers is only 35 days, the net cash flow would increase by approximately 14,000 €.

Besides showing you the biggest risk factors of your project and their impact on your outcome, the tornado diagram also provides a vital insight for you. From our experience, most of the time project teams are concerned about factors, which do not have a huge impact on the forecast at all. Being present at a project meeting of a big software company we once could observe a 2 hour conversation about who is supposed to have a company mobile phone and who is not. The team members argued that this issue is of importance because it is a big cost driver. After the meeting we ran the tornado tool. It stated that the uncertainty about how many people will get a company mobile phone did hardly have any impact on the value at all. Bottom line: a lot of time and effort is spent analyzing factors like these, although it would be more efficient to spend this time and effort on the assumptions that really matter. The barber probably would also have guessed by now that e.g. "Number of new customers due to marketing campaign" would have the greatest impact on the net cash flow. However, due to the tornado diagram he knows that the minimum as well as the maximum value of "Number of new customers due to marketing campaign" would only change the forecast by +/- 1,000 €, compared to the forecasted net cash flow, which would vary by more than +/- 10,000 € depending on the "Latency due to friction".

Making use of the sensitivity analysis gives you the advantage of assuring the likelihood of your results, identifying crucial risk factors, and knowing your impact on the results. "But what is to be done with the new insight provided to me by the tornado diagram?" you might ask. This is an obvious question. It is nice to know, what the crucial risk factors of the project are and see their impact on your results, but how can you make use of the tornado diagram and apply its results?

■ HOW TO APPLY THE RESULTS OF TORNADO DIAGRAM

The answer is quite simple. You would like to further investigate the assumptions, which appear at the top of the diagram, in the hope of reducing its uncertainties and therefore its impact on your target forecast.

As described earlier in this chapter, the assumption 'Latency due to friction' appears at the top of the barber's tornado diagram. Because it is an assumption, a certain level of uncertainty is still implied. The barber is supposed to spend more time and effort in reducing this uncertainty because of its great impact on the target forecast. Analyzing the assumption in more detail and reducing the uncertainty will lead to more certainty in the results and a less risky project. It is of importance that the barber directs his effort on the assumptions, which have the biggest impact on the results and not on assumptions at the bottom of the tornado diagram, such as "Frequency" or "Number of customers".

The barber reflects on what he has done so far. A while ago he noticed a decline of his customers which he based on decreasing customer's satisfaction. Instead of inactively watching his business run down, he thought about a new marketing campaign, which will increase the customers' satisfaction as well as already existing potential new customers. By using the Influence Matrix, creating the financial model and analyzing the results with sensitivity analysis he was able to forecast the success of his marketing campaign and also to compare this scenario to his current course and speed.

Afterword

"In some cases, the committees were categorically rejecting any investment where the benefits were primarily "soft" ones. Important factors [...] were being ignored in the evaluation process because they were considered immeasurable"[4]. This is a common behavior, when decision-makers undertake projects or investments, which include qualitative values. However, this book illustrated how using Business Case Analysis helps to overcome the problem of measuring soft or qualitative benefits to pave the way for your budget.

Following the three-step approach of creating an Influence Matrix, building the financial model, and performing a sensitivity analysis enables you to measure benefits such as customer satisfaction, image, quality or innovation. While the Influence Matrix visualizes the complexity of the decision problem, the financial model quantifies the elements of the decision problem and the sensitivity analysis identifies the probability of the results and possible risk factors. Capturing the complexity of a problem and possessing the ability to quantify the so called "intangibles" or "immeasurable values" enables organizations like yours to take these factors into consideration when undertaking new projects or investments. Taking these soft benefits into consideration shifts the ventures of your organization to a completely new level. By concentrating on qualitative values your organization will be able to stand out from the competition and is able to create a competitive advantage.

Concentrating on qualitative values and being able to quantify them in monetary terms will become more and more essential in future business. People, who are aware of this fact, are able to prepare themselves, handle the upcoming challenges, and look forward to a successful economic future.

---

4 Hubbard, 2007, p. 4.

Notes

1] Hubbard, D. W., How to Measure Anything, 1st edition, New Jersey, John Wiley and Sons, 2007.

2] Kettering, C. F., A problem well stated is a problem half solved, *http://thinkexist.com*, 2008.

3] Novo, J., Drilling Down, 3rd edition, Saint Petersburg, Book-locker.com, Inc., 2004.

4] Schmidt, M. J., Business Case Guide, 2nd edition, Boston, Solution Matrix Ltd., 2002.

Table of Figures

This appendix includes 30 different Influence Matrices for 10 industries. Purchasing-, Marketing-, Product Development-, Production-, IT-, Human Resources-, Project Management-, Sales- and Finance Departments can find their specific Influence Matrix in this section and build the foundation for a successful Business Case Analysis.

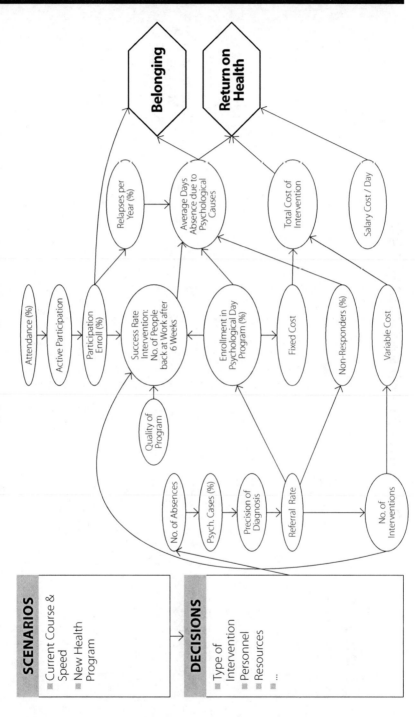

EMPLOYEE HEALTH PROGRAM

FREQUENT FLYER PROGRAM CRM

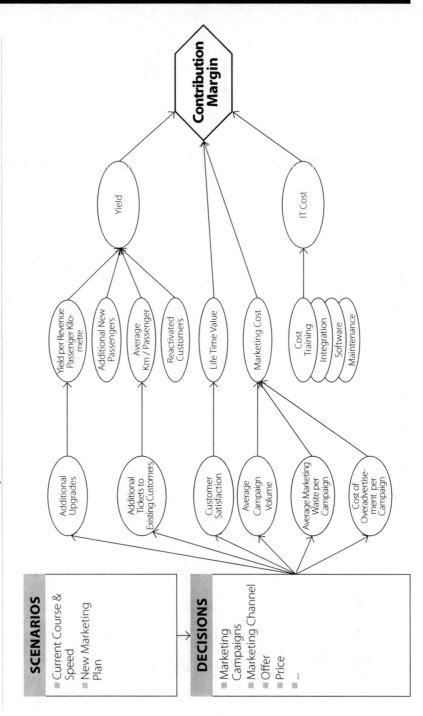

PRODUCT DEVELOPMENT

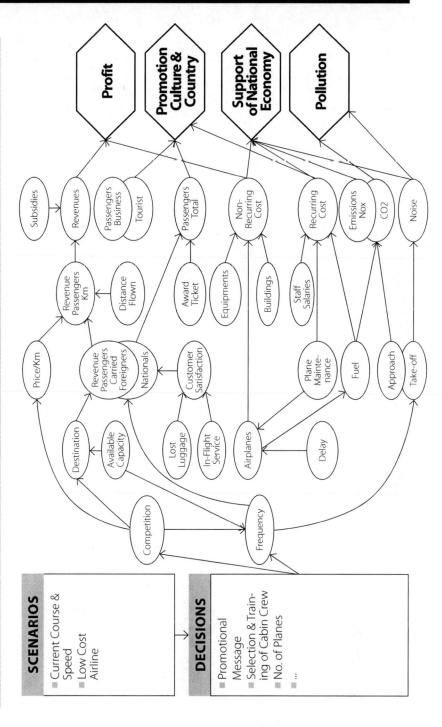

NEW DESCENT APPROACH

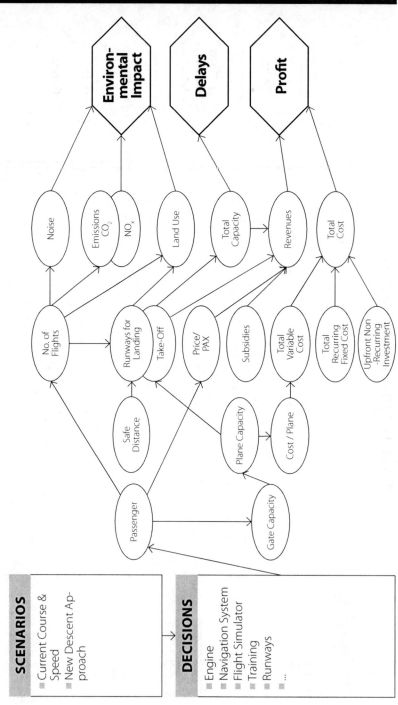

FUNDAMENTAL RESEARCH

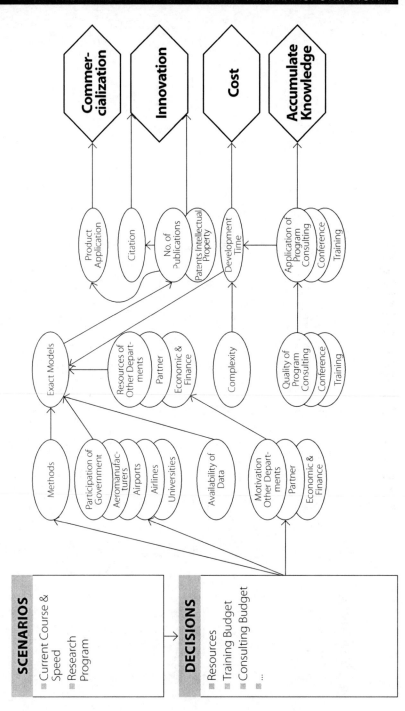

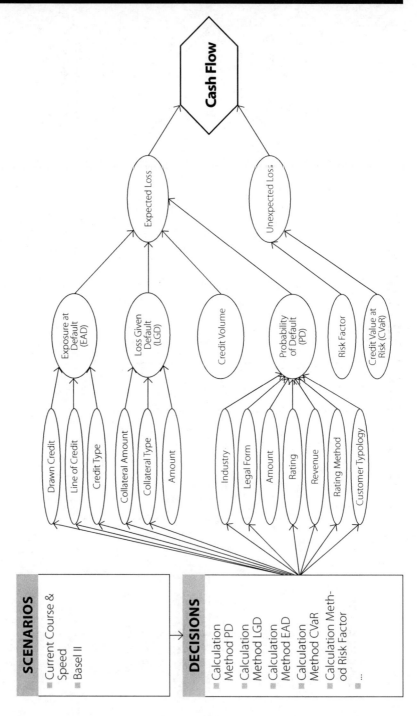

BASEL II CREDIT RISK MODEL

CROSS SELLING INSURANCE PRODUCTS

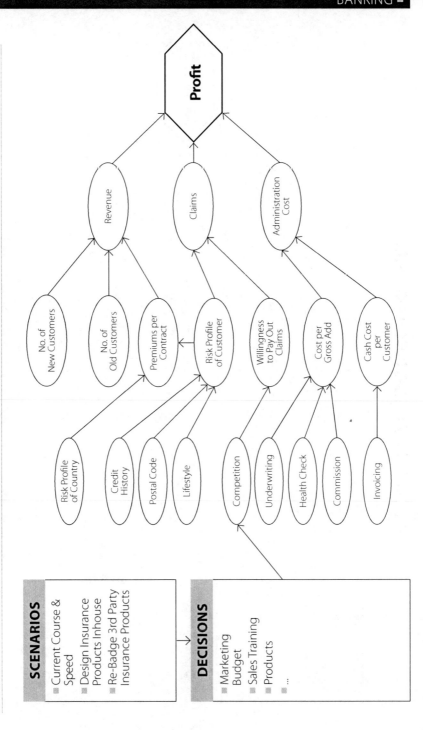

LOAN APPLICATION PROCESS

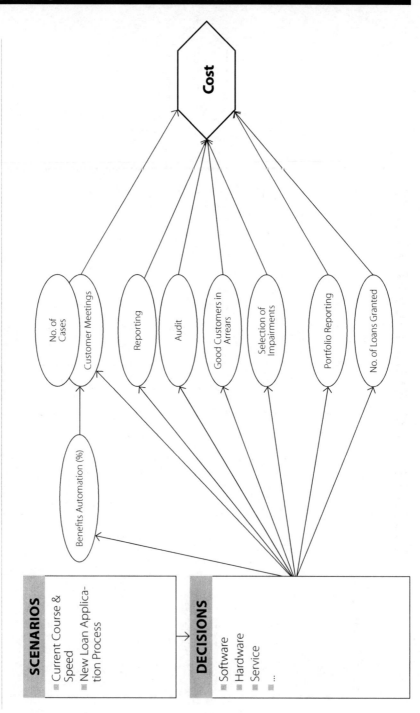

SCENARIOS
■ Current Course & Speed
■ New Loan Application Process

DECISIONS
■ Software
■ Hardware
■ Service
■ ...

Benefits Automation (%)

No. of Cases

Customer Meetings

Reporting

Audit

Good Customers in Arrears

Selection of Impairments

Portfolio Reporting

No. of Loans Granted

Cost

UP SELLING IN BANKING THROUGH CRM

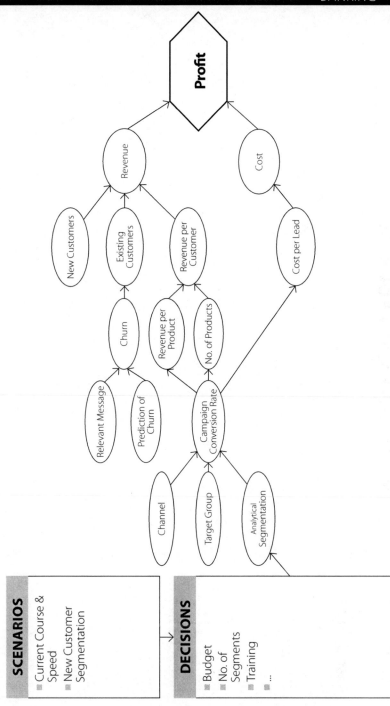

MARKETING & SALES PROGRAM

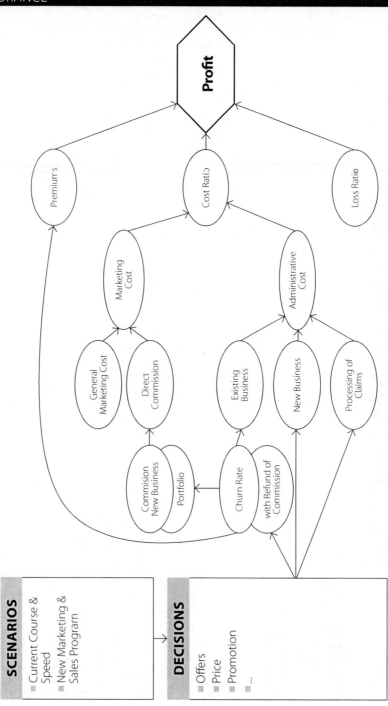

SOLVENCY II RISK MANAGEMENT

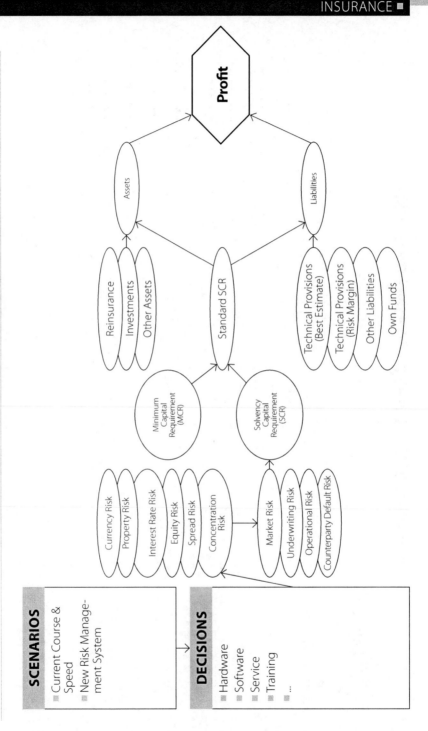

UNDERWRITING & RATE MAKING PROCESS

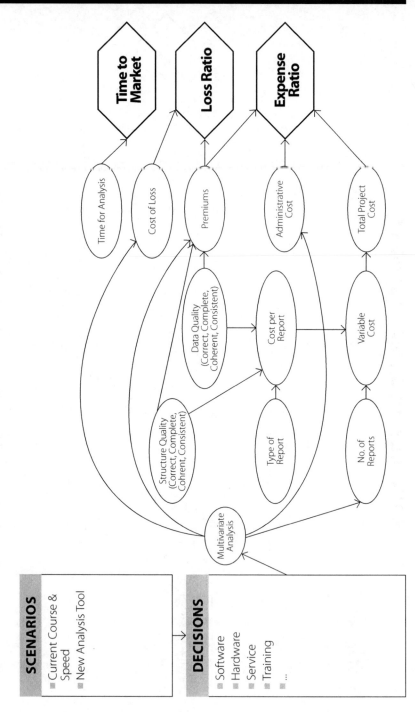

SCENARIOS

■ Current Course & Speed
■ New Analysis Tool

DECISIONS

■ Software
■ Hardware
■ Service
■ Training
■ ...

VALUE BASED INSURANCE MANAGEMENT

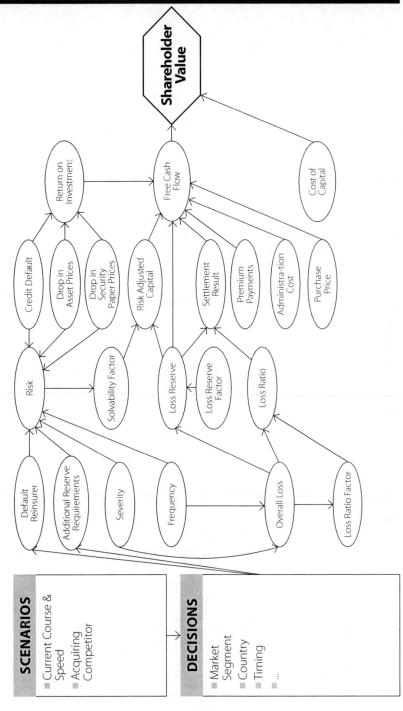

DATA CENTER PRICING STRATEGY

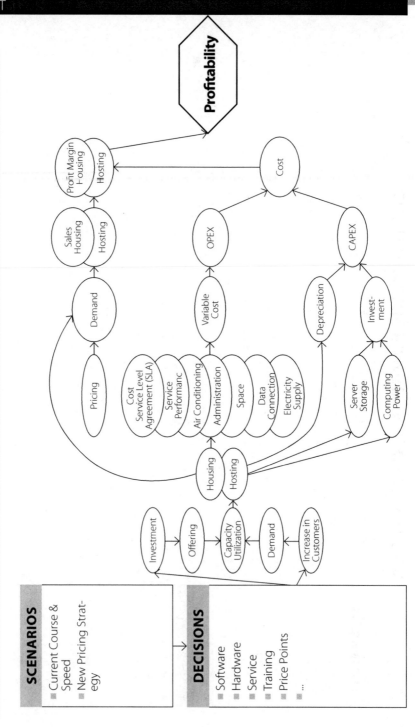

E-INVOICING SOLUTION

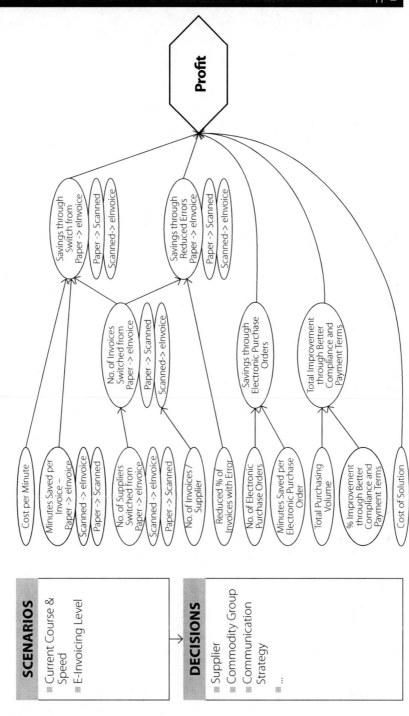

SOFTWARE START-UP ACQUISITION

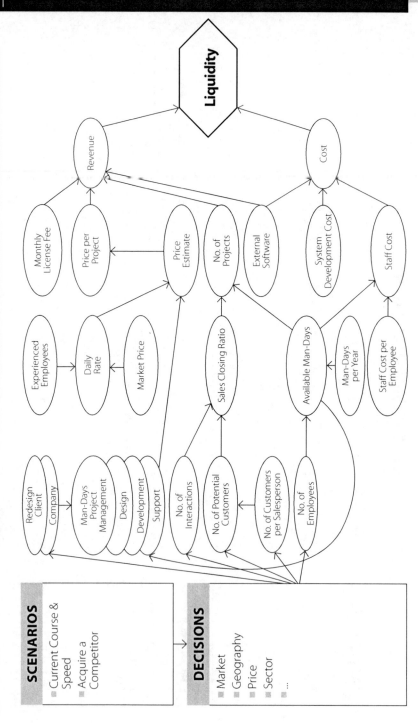

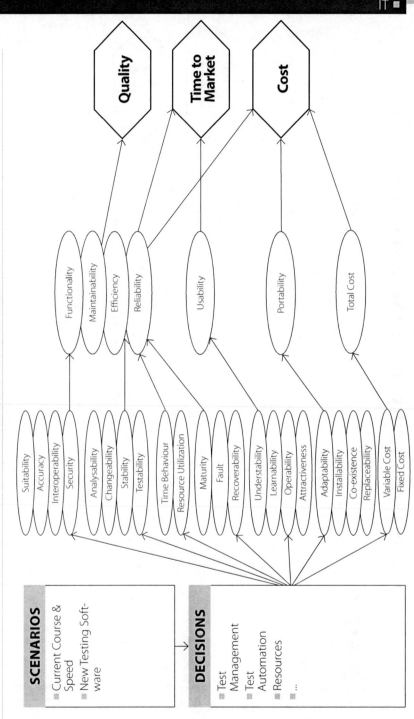

SOFTWARE TESTING

INTEGRATED CIRCUIT PRODUCTION PROCESS

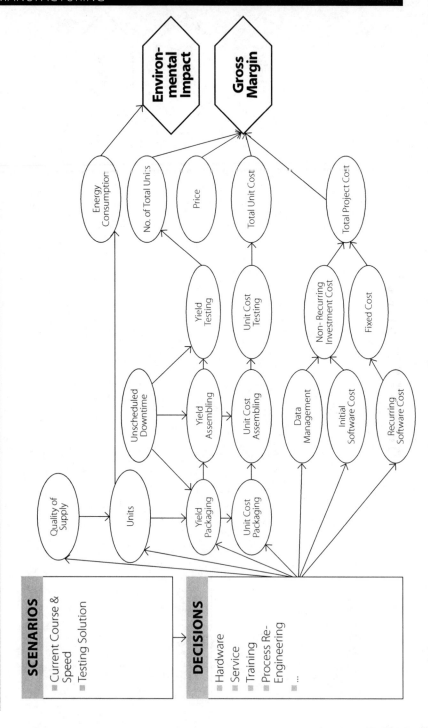

MANUFACTURING EXECUTION SYSTEM (MES)

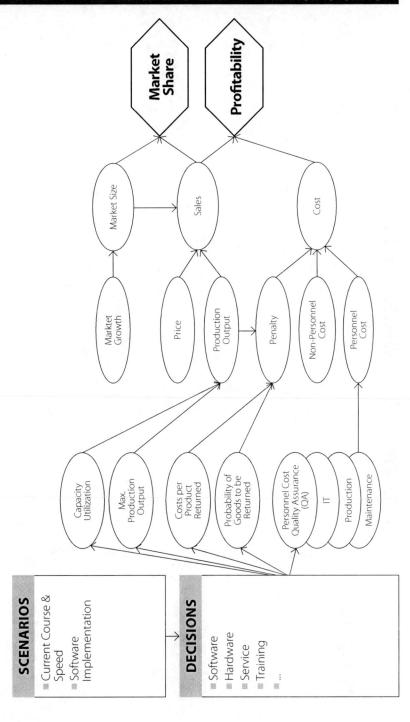

NEW PRODUCT DEVELOPMENT I

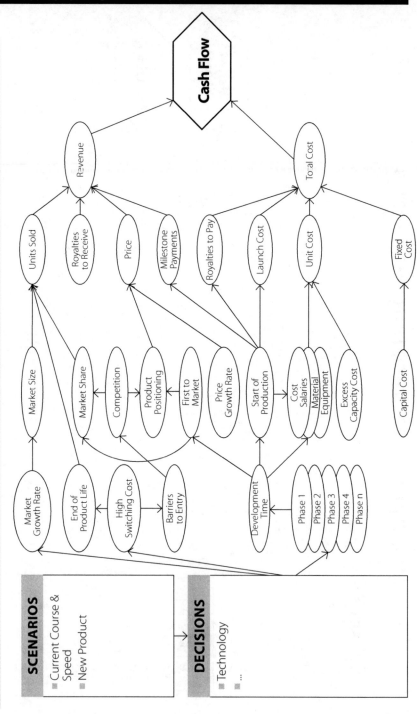

NEW PRODUCT DEVELOPMENT II

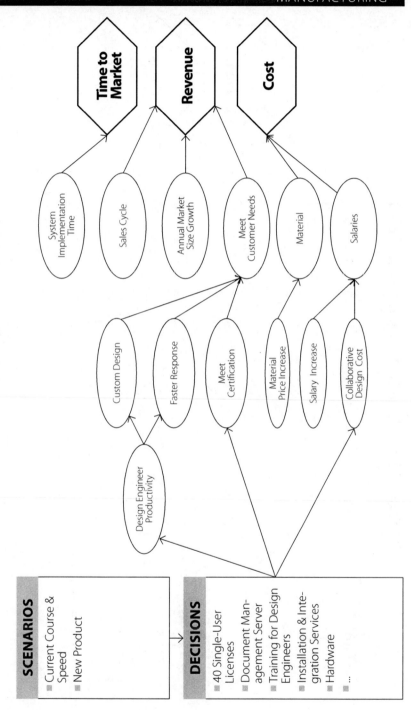

PRODUCT PORTFOLIO MANAGEMENT

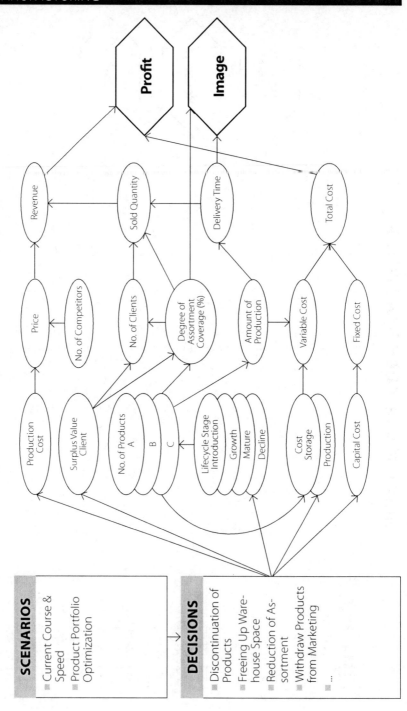

PURCHASING PLATFORM

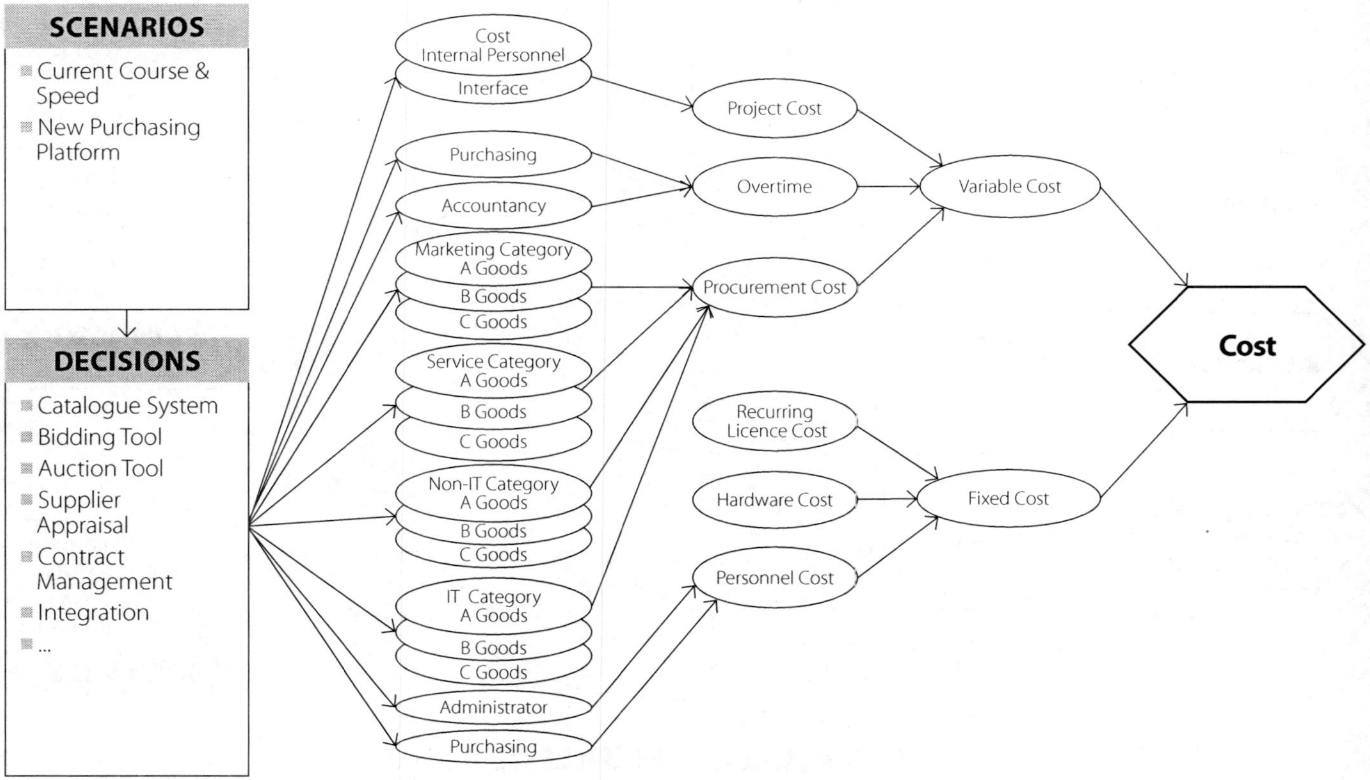

Cost

Variable Cost

Fixed Cost

Project Cost
Overtime
Procurement Cost
Recurring Licence Cost
Hardware Cost
Personnel Cost

Cost Internal Personnel
Interface
Purchasing
Accountancy
Marketing Category A Goods
B Goods
C Goods
Service Category A Goods
B Goods
C Goods
Non-IT Category A Goods
B Goods
C Goods
IT Category A Goods
B Goods
C Goods
Administrator
Purchasing

SCENARIOS

■ Current Course & Speed
■ New Purchasing Platform

DECISIONS

■ Catalogue System
■ Bidding Tool
■ Auction Tool
■ Supplier Appraisal
■ Contract Management
■ Integration
■ ...

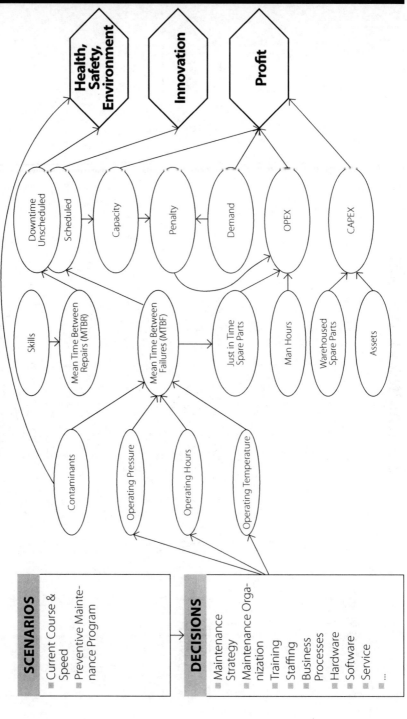

PREVENTIVE MAINTENANCE

E-GOVERNMENT PROGRAM

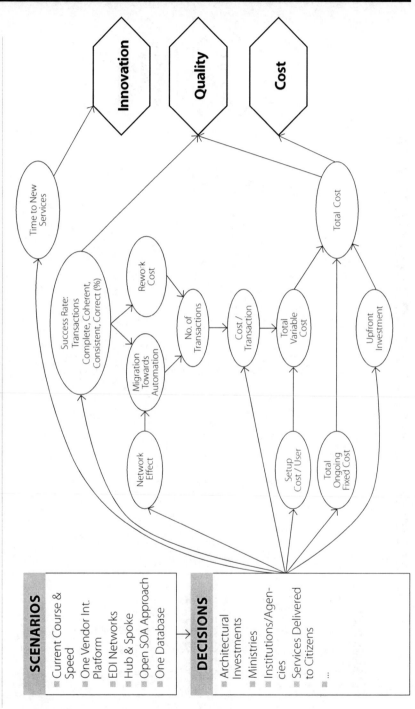

ADVERTISING AGENCY VALUE ADD FOR CUSTOMER

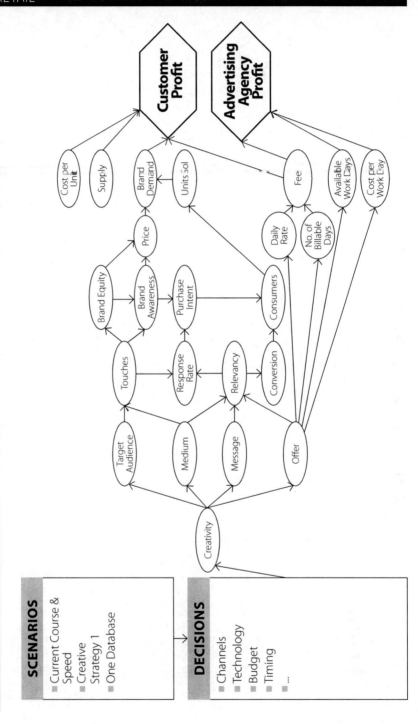

ADVERTISING AGENCY REORGANIZATION

SCENARIOS
▪ Current Course & Speed
▪ Creation of Client Service Function

DECISIONS
▪ Timing
▪ Qualification Re-quirements
▪ Content of Training
▪ ...

MOBILE OPERATOR CALL QUALITY

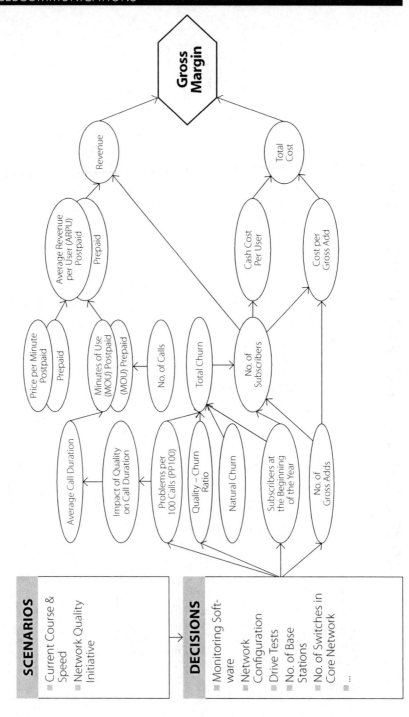

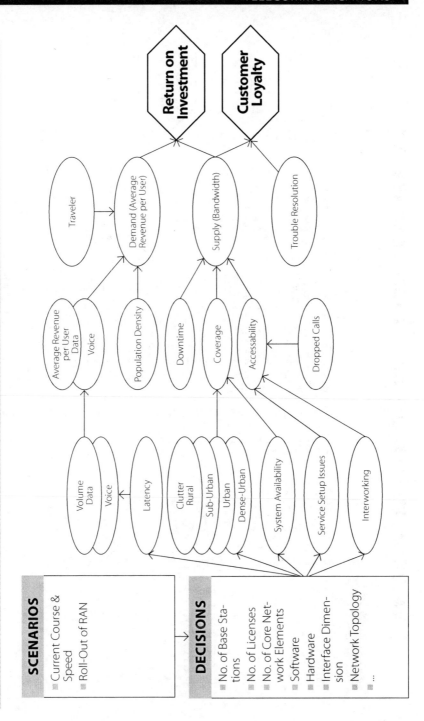

RADIO ACCESS NETWORK

VALUE BASED TELECOMMUNICATION MANAGEMENT

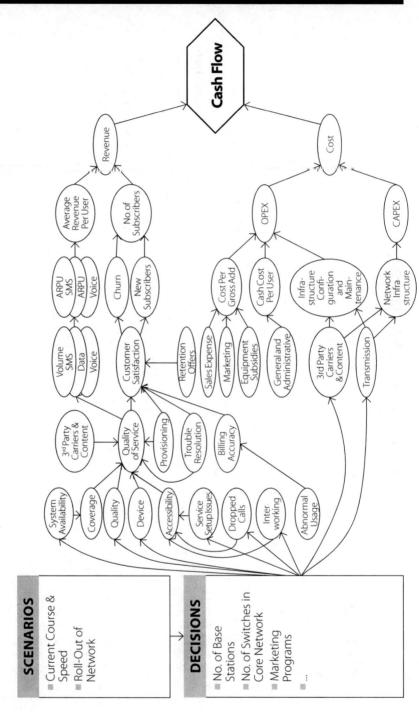

NORMAL DISTRIBUTION

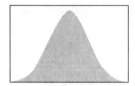

Normal

The normal distribution describes many natural phenomena such as IQs, people's heights, the inflation rate, or errors in measurements. It is a continuous probability distribution. The parameters for the normal distribution are mean and standard deviation.

There are three conditions underlying the normal distribution:
1) Some value of the unknown variable is the most likely (the mean of the distribution).
2) The unknown variable could as likely be above or below the mean (symmetrical about the mean).
3) The unknown variable is more likely to be close to the mean than far away. Of the values of a normal distribution, approximately 68% are within one standard deviation of the mean.

TRIANGULAR DISTRIBUTION

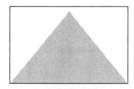

Triangular

The triangular distribution is commonly used when you know the minimum, maximum, and most likely values. For example, you could describe the number of cars sold per week when past sales show the minimum, maximum, and most likely number of cars sold. It is a continuous probability distribution. The parameters for the triangular distribution are minimum, likeliest, and maximum.

There are three conditions underlying the triangular distribution:
1) The minimum value is fixed.
2) The maximum value is fixed.
3) The most likely value falls at a point between the minimum and maximum values, forming a triangular shaped distribution, which shows that values near the minimum and maximum are less likely to occur than those near the most likely value.

UNIFORM DISTRIBUTION

Uniform

In the uniform distribution, all values between the minimum and maximum are equally likely to occur. It is a continuous probability distribution. The parameters for the uniform distribution are minimum and maximum.

There are three conditions underlying the uniform distribution:
1) The minimum value is fixed.
2) The maximum value is fixed.
3) All values between the minimum and maximum are equally likely to occur.

LOGNORMAL DISTRIBUTION

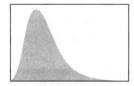

Lognormal

The lognormal distribution is widely used in situations where values are positively skewed (where most of the values occur near the minimum value) like in financial analysis for security valuation or in real estate for property valuation. It is a continuous probability distribution.

Financial analysts have observed that the stock prices are usually positively skewed, rather than normally (symmetrically) distributed. Stock prices exhibit this trend because the stock price cannot fall below the lower limit of zero but may increase to any price without limit. Similarly, real estate prices illustrate positive skewness since property values cannot become negative. The parameters for the lognormal distribution are mean and standard deviation.

There are three conditions underlying the lognormal distribution:
1) The unknown variable can increase without bound, but is confined to a finite value at the lower limit.
2) The unknown variable exhibits a positively skewed distribution.
3) The natural logarithm of the unknown variable will yield a normal curve.

Textbook Trialware

Free 140-day Trial of Crystal Ball Software Compliments of the Crystal Ball Education Alli

KEEP THIS CARD!!

See instructions to download
Oracle Crystal Ball software

ORACLE®

Please be aware that the Oracle download process can change and is beyond our control. If you would like instructions on how to download your copy of the Oracle Crystal Ball software please visit: http://www.solutionmatrix.com/crystalball.html

1. Visit http://www.oracle.com/technology/products/bi/crystalball
2. Click on the Free Download link
3. Download and install Oracle Crystal Ball software
4. Enter the information below when prompted

username: Ritter Rottgers 1st Edition 9783000263071
serial number: 27A858C6-9594B62D-1FD45ABC-A7FB4993

Lightning Source UK Ltd.
Milton Keynes UK
UKOW041525160412

190843UK00010B/139/P